The PARABLES *of*
KAHLIL GIBRAN

The PARABLES *of*
KAHLIL GIBRAN

An Interpretation of
His Writings and His Art

by ANNIE SALEM OTTO

THE CITADEL PRESS · NEW YORK

Acknowledgment is hereby extended to Alfred A. Knopf,
Inc. for permission to reprint material from the follow-
books by Kahlil Gibran:

> A Tear and a Smile
> Jesus the Son of Man
> Nymphs of the Valley
> Prose Poems
> The Earth Gods
> The Forerunner
> The Garden of the Prophet
> The Madman
> The Prophet
> The Wanderer
> Twenty Drawings
> Sand and Foam

Copyright 1918, 1919, 1920, 1923, 1926, 1928, 1931 by
Kahlil Gibran.
Copyright 1932, 1933, 1950, 1962 by Alfred A. Knopf,
Inc.

Acknowledgment is hereby extended to Alfred A. Knopf,
Inc. for permission to reprint from:

> This Man From Lebanon by Barbara Young,
> Copyright 1945, by Barbara Young.
> Merely Players by C. F. Bragdon, Copyright
> 1929, by Claude Bragdon.

FIRST EDITION

Preface

KAHLIL GIBRAN WROTE several books of parables. This book considers primarily those which he wrote directly in English. Gibran, an artist as well as a poet, employed the parabolic method in his prose and art. By definition the parable is a fictitious narrative of events in human life or a process in nature by which a spiritual truth is illustrated or enforced. This book concerns itself, therefore, with the interpretation of the spiritual lesson of Gibran's parables in both his writings and his art.

A description of Gibran's life is presented, with the emphasis on the experiences which formulated his ideas concerning man in society, ideas which are reflected in his writings and art. A criterion, consisting of five principles taken from Francis L. Filas' book, *The Parables of Jesus*, is presented as the basis for interpretation. First, the parable, being a comparison, is presented in the two terms of its comparison, the fictional narrative and the spiritual reality or lesson. Second, minute details are considered as secondary details and therefore are not given significance. Third, literary expressions which are used to render an emotional effect may be dropped without changing the imagery or the spiritual lesson of the parable. Fourth, parables are vague and demand an *a priori* knowledge from the reader. The final consideration involves a word of caution concerning an "apparent" conclusion which only serves for added reflection. Gibran's parables do not necessarily include all five principles, but they follow the definition of the parable and partake of at least two or more principles. The parabolic approach to his art describes the intended movement of his subjects, which movement suggests the spiritual lessons of the drawing.

Gibran's parables exemplify the suffering, misunderstandings, and longings of men. He points to the importance of harmonious relationship among men. However, he prescribes no consistent rules of conduct. He emphasizes only the desperate need for man's awareness of the inner spiritual powers which can span the distances between men. It is a kind of "communion in space," a "realm of consciousness" which unites all men regardless of race. "This is kinship, only this," is Gibran's final conclusion.

Acknowledgments

My DEEPEST APPRECIATION goes to Dr. Alvice W. Yeats, Dr. Harry L. Frissell, and Dr. Claude B. Boren. Specifically, I thank Dr. Yeats for his patience and his kind understanding in allowing me the freedom to express my ideas, Dr. Frissell for his constructive criticism that aided me immensely in the proper organization of my manuscript, and Dr. Boren for his penetrating questions which, although painful at times, helped me to clarify my position. I also wish to thank Mr. Jerome A. Hock, assistant professor of art, for the photographic reproductions of Gibran's art, and Miss Mildred Hansen, for the translation of the French article on Gibran.

A. S. O.

Beaumont, Texas
May, 1962

Contents

Illustrations

The PARABLES *of*
KAHLIL GIBRAN

1

Biography of Kahlil Gibran

KAHLIL GIBRAN WAS born on January 6, 1883, in
Bsherri, Lebanon.[1] Lebanon is an ancient country rich in
legend and Biblical inference. It is the traditional birth-
place of Tammuz and Ishtar,[2] the home of the ancient
Phoenicians, the setting of the *Song of Songs*, and the seat
of the Judaeo-Christian tradition. Lebanon is also a country
where some of the practices of everyday living are in direct
contradiction to the teachings of the religious sects within
its borders. It is this contradiction which gave impetus to
much of Gibran's early works and which comes into sharp
focus in his later works written in America.

The family of Gibran were Maronite Catholics.[3] Ka-

[1] The biographical facts are taken primarily from: Mikhail Naimy,
Kahlil Gibran: A Biography (New York: The Philosophical Library, 1950);
Barbara Young, *This Man from Lebanon* (New York: Alfred A. Knopf,
1945); Kahlil Gibran, *Kahlil Gibran: A Self-Portrait*, trans. and ed. Anthony R. Ferris (New York: The Citadel Press, 1959).

[2] Sir James George Frazer, *The Golden Bough* (New York: The Macmillan Company, 1947). Tammuz is a personified god who represents
the yearly decay and revival of life, and who annually died and rose again
from the dead. Ishtar, his sister, is the goddess of earth and heaven.

[3] The Maronite Cathloics affiliated with the Roman Catholic church
in 1736. However, they retained the tradition of the marriage of priests.

mila, the mother, was the daughter of a Maronite priest. She was a widow with a small child, Peter, when Kahalil Gibran, the poet's father, first heard her singing in her father's garden and determined to marry her. Besides Kahlil,[4] Kamila was to bear two daughters, Marianna and Sultana. She was described as being quiet, soft-spoken, poised, intelligent, linguistically adept, and "wise beyond the wisdom of many mothers."[5] Early in Kahlil's life Kamila recognized the potentialities of the rebellious child that was born to her. She said, "My son is outside psychology."[6] He was "unpredictable and difficult, tender over a broken flower at one moment, and the next raging like a young lion because of some imposition of authority upon him."[7] Of his early childhood, Gibran said,

> I was really not a nice boy, but it was because I was restless. I felt strange and lost. I could not find my way. But my mother knew it though I never told her. I did not need to tell her.[8]

Kamila Gibran took great interest in her child. The young Kahlil was tutored at home, learning to speak Arabic, French, and English. Kamila sang to him for long hours, filled his imagination with the folk-lore and legends of the Arabs—the exciting tales of Haroun-al-Raschid and Abu N'Was and *The Arabian Nights*. To add to the child's wonder, his father took him for long walks to visit the ancient villages of Baalbek, Homs, and Hamah. Sometimes they spent the night in a shepherd's tent " 'on top of Cedar

----

[4] Kahlil Gibran was named Gibran Khalil Gibran. While attending school in America, and at the suggestion of his teacher, he dropped the use of his first name and changed the spelling of Khalil.

[5] Young, p. 9.

[6] *Ibid.*, p. 145.

[7] *Ibid.*

[8] *Ibid.*

Mountain with the moon and stars above you, the peaceful
sheep and grey hills about you, and the sea below—how
very witching it was.' "[9] It was no wonder then that many
times, especially during his subsequent illness, living in the
hurry and scurry of metropolitan New York, Gibran was
filled with nostalgia for Lebanon and the joyful peace and
quiet it represented to him.

Also in Lebanon was a priest named Father Yusef,
who visited Bsherri in his travels from town to town. It was
of Father Yusef that Gibran said,

> *From him I learned to know God and the angels
> . . . It was his closeness to God . . . through him I was
> feeling the love of God. He did not tell me things I
> learned in the little church, but about the things in the
> above-world, things I could neither see nor hear, but
> that I could feel in my heart.*[10]

Gibran tried to express these inner experiences early in
his childhood. In the winter he fashioned strange unchild-
like figures in the snow, and the neighbors passed by and
admired them. In the spring he collected stones, hewed
them and built small churches and cathedrals. When he was
able to write, "he wrote furiously, page after page, only to
read and then to tear into pieces. 'It was never what I
wanted to say,' "[11] Gibran said. Soon he was painting and
drawing pictures, which were also destroyed as soon as they
were completed, because " 'they were never like what I saw
when my eyes were dark.' "[12]

Even as a child Gibran's art was the expression of his
inner feelings toward life experiences. Once when he was

[9] Naimy, p. 43.
[10] Young, pp. 96-97.
[11] *Ibid.*, p. 8.
[12] *Ibid.*

punished by the priest for not reading his Syriac lesson well, he drew a picture of what looked like a " 'sleeping donkey with a priest's cap on its head, and a book dangling from one ear and a feed-sack from the other.' "[13] At another time Gibran took a piece of charcoal and drew on the wall of his home what appeared to be a house with a sad girl sitting in front of it. Although the picture was not very clear, Gibran's father recognized in the drawing the awareness of the young Kahlil of his mother's sadness. The parents had quarreled bitterly before the sensitive boy.

Gibran's family was poor. The father did very little work. He spent most of his time visiting his friends, drinking arak[14] and coffee, and smoking cigarettes. One day Peter, dissatisfied with the conditions at home, told his mother that he wanted to go to America. He had heard that America was a land filled with opportunities for those who were willing to take advantage-of them. He could go to Boston, where relatives and many Lebanese friends lived. Peter promised to support the family, educate his brother Kahlil, and send money home to his stepfather. Kamila agreed that Peter could go to America, but she and the children were to go also.

In June, 1894, the family, consisting of Kamila Gibran, Peter, Kahlil, Marianna, and Sultana, came to the United States and settled in a small apartment in Boston's China-town. Chinatown, with its closely built tenement houses and its garbage-littered streets, was quite a contrast to the little village that nestled against the side of Cedar Mountain and faced the open sea.

For two and a half years, Gibran attended school in Boston. His English teacher recognized the precocity of the

[13] Naimy, p. 21.
[14] Arak is a national drink in Lebanon. It is distilled from grapes, and when mixed with water turns the color of milk.

child, and she gave him many books to read. His drawing teacher, delighted with his work, showed his drawings to a painter who said that Gibran was a little artist. The painter, whose name is not recorded, invited Gibran to his studio and later asked the young boy to pose for him, paying him with paints instead of money.

In 1896, Gibran insisted on returning alone to Lebanon to complete his education in Arabic literature. " 'I knew that I could only be what I had it in me to be if I went back to my country.' "[15]

Gibran's extensive writings on religious themes may be traced back in part to the rigor of his religious training in Lebanon. During his four years at Madrasat Al-Hikmat, School of Wisdom,[16] Gibran was compelled to attend church twice a day. He later said to himself of this experience,

> *Surely you have prayed enough to last you to the end of your days, and hence forth you shall not enter a church as a worshipper; for the Jesus you love so dearly is not found in churches. Many are the places of worship, but few indeed are those who worship in Spirit and in truth.*[17]

Gibran studied a variety of subjects outside the prescribed curriculum in classical Arabic literature. He studied medicine, international law, the history of religion, and music. During this period Gibran, at fifteen, wrote the first version of *The Prophet* in Arabic. He edited a literary and philosophical magazine, *Al-Hakikat* [The Truth], at sixteen. At seventeen, Gibran made his first appearance in

[15] Young, p. 54.
[16] Madrasat Al-Hikmat, Beirut, Lebanon, is presently known as College de la Sagesse.
[17] Naimy, p. 43.

print with a prose poem in a Mt. Lebanon newspaper. Also at seventeen, Gibran made imaginary drawings of several early Islamic poets of whom no portraits existed: Al Farid, Abu N'Was, Al Mutanabbi, and Avicinna. He made drawings of Ibn Khaldun, the historian; Ibn Sinna, the philosopher; and Khansa, a great Arabic woman poet.

In 1901 Gibran graduated from Al-Hikmat with high honors. He visited Greece, Italy, and Spain en route to Paris to study art. During his stay in Paris, Gibran wrote *Spirits Rebellious* in Arabic. In this book Gibran became the first Arabic writer who openly and bitterly condemned the evils of the Church, the injustice of Justice, the sheiks who exploited the people, and family traditions which forced the marriage of young girls to old men and to men whom they did not love. In the voices of his characters, Gibran urged the people to rise in protest and to throw off the yokes and fetters that bound them into unquestioned submission. He attempted to arouse in them an awareness of their ability to choose a different way of life. This attack on the existing authorities created an outrageous protest from the Turkish leaders, the Arab sheiks, and the clergy. They exhibited their authority by publicly burning the book in the market place of Beirut. At the same time, Gibran was exiled from his country and excommunicated from the Maronite Catholic Church for writing a book that was "dangerous, revolutionary, and poisonous to youth."[18]

In 1903 Gibran was called from Paris to Boston to the bedside of his mother. Kamila remained bedridden for fifteen months before she died. During his mother's illness, Sultana, Gibran's sixteen-year-old sister, also died. A few months later Gibran's beloved half-brother Peter died. All three died of tuberculosis. Their deaths were a terrible shock to Gibran. The mother and four children were very

18 Young, p. 185.

close and dear to one another. The close family relationship was derived not only from their Arabic heritage[19] but also from the deeply felt and overtly expressed love that each shared with the other. The family had made many sacrifices for Kahlil. He was always encouraged to continue his studies; never was he asked to help support the family, regardless of their meager circumstances. When there were only Gibran and Marianna left, Marianna began to sew for others, insisting that Gibran not give up painting and writing. Before his works began to sell, however, Gibran worked at book binding, earning a little money to add to his sister's small income.

In the course of the next five years, Gibran painted and wrote profusely in Arabic. He rewrote *The Prophet* again in Arabic. His pictures began to attract public attention. An exhibition was held at the Studio of Fred Holland Day, a well-known photographer and Gibran's first patron, in January, 1904. One month later an exhibition was held at the Cambridge School, a private educational institution owned and operated by Mary Haskell, who became Gibran's close friend and benefactress for the remainder of his life. A third exhibition of Gibran's drawings was held in Fred Holland Day's studio; the building burned and the entire collection of drawings was destroyed. Gibran was saddened at the time, but later he said that he was glad because now he realized the drawings were all green work drawn by a "green artist."

In 1908 Gibran returned to Paris, visiting London along the way, to resume his work in art. Gibran studied at the Académie Julien and at the Ecole des Beaux Arts. He met and made portraits of many distinguished persons in Paris: Auguste Rodin, French sculptor; Henri de Rochefort,

[19] Sania Hamady, *Temperament and Character of the Arab* (New York: Twayne Publishers, 1960), p. 28.

French journalist and political leader; Achille Claude De-
bussy, French composer; Maurice Maeterlinck, Belgian
writer; and Edmond Rostand, French dramatic poet.
Gibran exhibited twice in the Paris Solon. Also in 1908,
Gibran received information that his exile had been re-
manded when an agreement with a new government in
Turkey had pardoned all exiles.

Gibran returned to Boston in the spring of 1910. His
finances began to improve, from the sale of his books and
drawings. In the winter of 1920, he moved to New York
City and took residence at 51 West Tenth Street, the first
studio building ever to be built in this country for the exclu-
sive use of painters and writers. Gibran lived in this building
until his death.

In 1914 Gibran exhibited at the Montrose Galleries,
New York. In 1917, exhibitions were held at the Knoedler
Galleries, New York, and at the Doll and Richards Galleries, Boston. Between 1917 and 1922, Gibran rewrote The
Prophet, still in Arabic. He wrote several Arabic books:
Broken Wings, in novel form; The Tempests, prose poem;
the Book of Tears and Laughter, short essays and prose
poems; Nymphs of the Valley, short stories; and Processions, a book length narrative poem in strict Arabic rhyme
and rhythm. A volume was published called Al Badayih wal
Tarayiff (Beautiful and Rare Sayings), in which were included drawings of the early Islamic poets and writers,
drawn from imagination at seventeen. All these books have
been translated into English by Arabic writers, except The
Prophet, which was finally written by Gibran directly in
English after a labor of five years. Al Badayih wal Tarayiff is
still in Arabic only.

Gibran contributed to several Arabic newspapers during this period, one of which was As-Sayeh, the Traveller.
On April 20, 1920, an entertainment was held by the pub-

lisher of *As-Sayeh*. Several Arab poets and writers attended. During the course of the evening, the poets and writers decided to band together in order to unify their efforts in the service of the Arabic language and literature. Eight days later, at a meeting held in Gibran's studio, eight of the men met and formally organized *Arrabitah*, the Pen-Bond. The members were A. Haddad, N. Haddad, Elias Atallah, W. Catzeflis, N. Arida, Rl Ayoub, Kahlil Gibran, and Mikhail Naimy. The purpose of the *Arrabitah* was to modernize Arabic literature in order to give it new life. The poets did not want to break away completely from the literature of the ancients, but they felt that the tendency to keep language and literature within the narrow limits of conformity in form and substance was a most pernicious tendency, and if left unopposed would soon lead to decay.[20] The active membership was limited to ten. The *Arrabitah* published the works of its own members and other Arab writers that they considered worthy. Efforts were made to encourage the translations of masterpieces of world literature into Arabic.

The works of the writers were reprinted in anthologies and school texts. The fame of *Arrabitah* spread throughout the Arabic speaking world. Groups of writers banded together and took the name of *Arrabitah* in Alleppo and Damascus, Syria, in Beirut and Tripoli, Lebanon, and in Cairo, Egypt. The members contributed poems and short stories to other Arabic newspapers and magazines. As the fame of *Arrabitah* grew, the fame of their leader Kahlil Gibran increased everywhere among the millions of Arabs who read or who heard of Gibran.

A story is told of an American lady who was traveling in Lebanon, and meeting a young Lebanese poet said to him, "I know a countryman of yours in New York—Kahlil

[20] Naimy, p. 156.

Gibran. Do you know him?" And the young poet replies, "Madame, do I ask you if you know Shakespeare?"[21]

Mikhail Naimy, Gibran's close friend and biographer, writes of Gibran's encounter with the work of Friedrich Nietzsche. Nietzsche's works bear a direct influence on Gibran's thinking during this period. Later, under Nietzschean influence, Gibran developed a new style of the prose poem both in Arabic and English. Gibran extolled the imagination of Nietzsche which created the Superman. Gibran said,

> With one leap it [the imagination] would reach the core of life, divest it of all excrescences, then burn these excrescences and fling their ashes into the eyes of those who brought them into being. So must all imaginations be.[22]

Gibran became acquainted with the works of Nietzsche after he had completed *Broken Wings*. The book was greeted by the Arab world as an innovation in that it was the first work by an author that broke away from the imitation of the old classics. One ancient mode of story telling was the lament at the breaking up of the camp. Then the lonely lover returned and began his poem describing the deserted scene and the loss of his love. The descriptive words varied, but the motif remained the same. *Broken Wings* is a direct description of life as experienced by Gibran during his stay in Lebanon. In the book, Gibran expressed his disappointment over the weakness of his countrymen who quietly surrendered their own power to the traditional authority of the clergy. He disdained this weakness in mankind, and Nietzsche's brilliance was added fuel to his disturbed and lonely spirit. Gibran began to write parables and prose poems in an effort to awaken his

21 Young, p. 31.
22 Naimy, p. 119.

people to their plight. In a parable titled "The Grave Diggers,"[23] Gibran has the Phantom of Death, who calls himself The Mad God, say to Abdallah, the slave of God,

> You cling with terror to the small circle of gifts from your ancestors, and your affliction is caused by your parents' bequest, and you will remain a slave of death until you become one of the dead. . .
> Your illusioned eyes see the people quivering before the tempests of life and you believe them to be alive, while in truth they have been dead since they were born. There were none to bury them, and the one good career for you is that of grave digger, and as such you may rid the few living of corpses heaped about their homes, the paths, and the churches.[24]

Gibran wrote copiously and vehemently under the influence of Nietzsche. In imitation of Nietzschean style, Gibran began to express himself directly to his readers instead of using fictitious characters. He also used the same lofty tone as Nietzsche in his endeavor to quicken his people into a new awareness. His writings became bitter and ironic. *The Madman*, 1918, Gibran's first English book of parables, expressed his inner bitterness at the existing relationships among men. In 1919, *Twenty Drawings*, a collection of Gibran's drawings, was published and even his art depicted the struggles of the inner life of the artist and poet. *The Forerunner*, published in 1920, contained parables and poems somewhat less bitter, but the disillusionment remained. Soon an incident occurred which revealed Gibran to himself and consequently created within him a new awakening and a new understanding of himself. The incident occurred at a time when Gibran's fi-

[23] Kahlil Gibran, *A Treasury of Kahlil Gibran*, trans. Anthony R. Ferris, (ed.) Martin L. Wolf (New York: The Citadel Press, 1958), p. 389.
[24] *Ibid.*, p. 390.

nances had improved. The sale of his books and drawings alleviated the poverty he and Marianna had suffered since the deaths of their mother, brother, and sister. Electrical outlets were installed in the apartment, a gas stove was purchased, and finally a telephone was installed. Gibran was beginning to be recognized in America as both an artist and poet. People began to express warm praise and affection for his work. He gloried in the praise heaped upon him. Gibran tried to justify people's estimates and expectations of him. However, there remained a silent struggle between his inner and outer selves.

One day in the summer of 1921, Gibran and three of his friends—Mikhail Naimy, A. Haddah, and Nassieb Arida—decided to take a vacation. They chose a small village some one hundred miles from New York. Cahoonize proved to be a small paradise surrounded by miles of forest, many lakes, and running streams. The friends were inseparable. They walked together, ate together, went to sleep, and rose from sleep at the same time. Naimy said,

> The people of the hamlet and the other vacationists in it nicknamed us "The Big Four"—a title given to the authors of the Versailles Treaty: the resemblance going no further than the number.[25]

One morning the four friends walked several miles to a waterfall. The rushing water, the majestic trees, the beauty of nature created a feeling of freedom, a kind of abandonment to the beauty of nature. They managed to cross the stream to a large flat rock. There they arranged themselves where they could face the waterfall, and they began to sing. The old folk songs of Syria and Lebanon were freely sung, not always in unison, but sung nevertheless. Soon it was time to return; the friends began to wend their way slowly

[25] Naimy, p. 169.

along the narrow paths. Gibran and Naimy, absorbed in conversation, fell a short distance behind the others. The conversation reached a certain point; then suddenly both were silent. Then with a shout of alarm Gibran cried aloud, "Mischa! Mischa, I am a false alarm."[26] Here began the true revelation of Gibran to himself. For when man can discover within himself what is false and what is true about himself, then truly there can be an awakening and consequently a right transformation. And certainly it is a great spirit that can recognize and declare its own deception. "I am a false alarm" is a beginning and an end.

Gibran now felt deeply the burden of his responsibilities. The ancient truth of another poet came to have more meaning for him.

> *Whoever would be a teacher of men let him begin by teaching himself before teaching others; and let him teach by example before teaching by word. For he who teaches himself and rectifies his own ways is more deserving of respect and reverence than he who would teach others and rectify their ways.*[27]

Thus Gibran set his aim toward rectifying his own ways, realizing that "Everything I have imprisoned in expression I must free by my deeds."[28] Gibran intensified his efforts, not only in his writings, but in his art. In 1922 Gibran held an exhibition at the Woman's City Club in Boston. In 1929 another exhibition was held at Hotel Brevoort in New York. During this period, Gibran met and made portraits of many eminent persons: Lady Augusta Gregory, Irish poet

[26] *Ibid.,* p. 171.

[27] *Ibid.,* p. 196. Attributed to Iman Ali, who was ruler of the Moslems 656 A.D. Additional information from R. A. Nicholson, *A Literary History of the Arabs* (New York: Cambridge University Press, 1956 ed.).

[28] Kahlil Gibran, *Sand and Foam* (New York: Alfred A. Knopf, 1926), p. 85.

and dramatist; Sarah Bernhardt, French actress; William Butler Yeats, Irish poet; Dr. Charles Eliot, English Bishop and author; Richard Le Galliene, English writer; Paul Bartlett, American sculptor; John Masefield, English author and poet; Edwin Markham, American poet; Abdul Baha, Persian Bahai leader; AE [George William Russell], Irish poet and painter; Laurence Housman, English author and illustrator; Johan Bojer, Norwegian novelist; Witter Bynner, American poet; Josephine Preston Peabody, American poet; and Alice Raphael, artist and writer of the "Introduction" to Gibran's Twenty Drawings. Gibran became recognized as an accomplished artist. Two original wash drawings and three pencil drawings are in the Metropolitan Museum, New York, and a number are in the Fogg Museum, Cambridge, Massachusetts, in the Brooklyn Museum, and in the Newark Museum. A collection of wash and pencil drawings is in the possession of Barbara Young, Gibran's literary executor. This collection has been exhibited widely in American cities, in England, and in Paris.

In 1923, after five long years of labor, Gibran's The Prophet was published, this time written by him directly in English. It is Gibran's masterpiece. The Prophet has been translated into twenty languages and approximately ten dialects. In the first year of publication, The Prophet sold a modest twelve hundred copies.[29] Acclaimed by word of mouth, the demand for copies has gradually accelerated until in recent years, The Prophet has sold from forty to ninety thousand copies annually. In 1957, the millionth copy was presented to Red Barber, who is not only a noted sportscaster but a lay reader in the Episcopal Church. Red Barber became interested in The Prophet when a friend gave it to him while he was in the hospital in 1948. Since

[29] The following information is contained in a letter from Alfred A. Knopf to Annie Salem Otto dated November 23, 1961.

then, Mr. Barber has made a practice of giving Gibran's inspirational book to his friends. "When a friend seems to be concerned about his children," says Barber, "I don't know anything better to do than give him a copy of *The Prophet* and ask him to read the section 'On Children' the first of every month."[30]

 Sand and Foam was published in 1926. It is a collection of aphorisms and poems. It is written as though a philosopher were gazing on the activities of humanity and making comments on the passing scenes. In 1928 *Jesus the Son of Man* was published. In this book Gibran delineates the lives of those who knew Jesus. Claude Bragdon in his book *Merely Players* devoted eight pages to Gibran. Bragdon says of Gibran's treatment of Jesus in *Jesus the Son of Man*:

> He chooses Jesus as the great exemplar and he is so eager that his readers should both see and understand Him, that he adopts the device of straining Jesus, so to speak, through the consciousness of His contemporaries, enemies and friends alike—each one a cloth of finer or coarser texture, in which some trait or aspect is netted, or on which it leaves an azure or crimson stain.[31]

 Gibran describes Jesus in the role of the great Liberator. Jesus attempted to break the traditional bondage which captivates the thoughts of men; but Paul reverted back to the prophetic teachings, and therefore, to the renewal of the chains of yesterdays. Jesus also showed men that love exists among them, even the mother of Judas could not deny that love.

[30] *Ibid.*
[31] C. F. Bragdon, *Merely Players* (New York: Alfred A. Knopf, 1929), p. 144.

Saba of Antioch says of Paul's teachings:

*He speaks not of Jesus, nor does he repeat His
words. He preaches the Messiah whom the prophets of
old had foretold.*

*We who knew Jesus and heard His discourses say
that He taught man how to break the chains of his
bondage that he might be free from his yesterdays.*

*But Paul is forging chains for the man of tomorrow.
He would strike with his own hammer upon the anvil
in the name of One whom he does not know.*[32]

The mother of Judas says of her son:

*I beg you question me no further about my son.
I loved him and I shall love him forevermore.*

*If love were in the flesh I would burn it out with
hot irons and be at peace. But it is in the soul,
unreachable. . .*

*Go to the mother of Jesus. The sword is in her heart
also; she will tell you of me, and you will understand.*[33]

In 1931 *The Earth Gods* was published. Gibran was
presented with the finished book two weeks before his
death. Gibran had a special feeling of tenderness for this
book. He had begun the writing of it in 1914, when he was
trying to express himself directly in English. He said, "It
was written out of the poet's hell—a process of child-birth
and child-bearing."[34]

The Wanderer, completed but still in manuscript at
the poet's death, was published in 1932. *The Garden of the
Prophet*, a companion to *The Prophet*, was not completed
at the time of Gibran's death. Barbara Young, his close

[32] Kahlil Gibran, *Jesus the Son of Man* (New York: Alfred A. Knopf,
1928), pp. 61-62.
[33] *Ibid.*, p. 204.
[34] Young, p. 113.

friend during the last seven years of Gibran's life, gathered
the fragments together and arranged them as a continuation
of the sayings of the prophet.

For the development of his gifts and for the understanding of himself, Gibran acknowledged his indebtedness
to women.

> Women opened the windows of my eyes and the
> doors of my spirit. Had it not been for the woman-
> mother, the woman-sister, and the woman-friend, I
> would have been sleeping among those who seek the
> tranquility of the world with their snoring.[35]

Gibran's first romance occurred during his student
days at Al-Hikmat. The love he felt for Selma Karamy and
the bitter disappointment at her forced marriage is told
in broken-hearted and sentimental outpourings in Broken
Wings. The tender wings of the soaring imagination of
youth in love were harshly broken by a corrupt bishop who
wished to marry Selma Karamy to his depraved nephew.
Selma's father happened to be a wealthy man, and the
bishop fostered the match in the hope of financial gain.
Gibran violently protested against the silent acquiescence of
the father and of the daughter to the demands of the bishop
who, Gibran said, went to church in the morning and spent
the remainder of the day pilfering from widows, orphans,
and simple-minded people.

> Human society has yielded for seventy centuries to
> corrupted laws until it cannot understand the meaning
> of superior and eternal laws. . . Spiritual disease is
> inherited from one generation to another until it be-
> comes a part of the people, who look upon it, not as a
> disease, but as a natural gift, showered by God on

[35] Kahlil Gibran: A Self-Portrait, p. 84.

Adam. If these people found someone free from the germs of this disease, they would think of him with shame and disgrace.[36]

Broken Wings was dedicated to Mary Haskell, who became Gibran's confidential editor of all his English books and to whom he referred as his guardian-angel.

Mary Haskell was the owner and operator of the Cambridge School for Girls. She met Gibran in 1904 in Fred Holland Day's studio, where Gibran held his first public exhibition. Impressed with Gibran's work, Miss Haskell invited Gibran to the School to lecture on art. This was the beginning of their close friendship. Mary Haskell made it possible for Gibran to return to Paris to continue his study. She bought his ticket and offered to send him seventy-five dollars each month as a "small gift from me as a token of love and appreciation of your rich talents."[37] Two years later, 1910, as Gibran stood alone on the deck of the ship that was returning him to America, he reflected on his lonely life. Comparing himself to the mystic William Blake, he wondered if he could marry a woman and impart to her some of his fiery imagination. Determined to attempt a conventional life, Gibran, on his arrival in Boston, sought Mary Haskell and after much circuitous conversation of Paris and his future plans said to Mary abruptly,

"Will you walk the road with me to the end?" With childlike simplicity and frankness entirely unarmed, and therefore able to disarm its opponent, Mary replied with another question, her voice and face still reflecting her bewilderment. "But are you clean, Kahlil?"[38]

[36] Kahlil Gibran, *Broken Wings*, trans. Anthony R. Ferris (New York: The Citadel Press, 1957), pp. 105-106.
[37] Naimy, p. 74.
[38] *Ibid.*, p. 105.

Gibran was stung and stunned. This question had only one meaning for him. The blow to his pride was unbearable. Angrily he thrust himself quickly out of Mary Haskell's presence and apartment. In a few days his anger subsided, but he decided to do nothing except to keep a strict silence about the entire affair. Not long afterwards, the mailman brought Gibran a letter from Mary Haskell. In it was the regular monthly check along with a loving letter written as if nothing had happened and nothing had changed. And it was to Mary Haskell that Gibran left at his death everything found in his studio: pictures, books, and objects of art.[39]

Another "woman-friend" to whom Gibran was indebted was Barbara Young, whose book *This Man from Lebanon* describes the last years of the poet's life. Of him she says,

> For seven years, and up to the very moment of his death, I had the joy and privilege of knowing Gibran as poet and painter, and as a close and beloved friend. Seven years of friendship and work; as he so generously said, we were "poets working together in Beauty's name."[40]

In 1923 Gibran's book *The Prophet* was read in the Church of St. Mark's in-the-Bouwerie in New York City. Barbara Young sat among the crowded congregation listening to the melodious but unusual phraseology of the words of Gibran. A short time later, she wrote to the poet expressing her admiration and enjoyment of his work. Gibran called her and invited her to come to his studio to talk about poetry and to see his pictures. At their first meeting they discovered an underlying affinity which only those who

---

[39] *Kahlil Gibran: A Biography*, p. 238. In addition to his sister, Marianna, his home town of Bsherri was to share in the royalties from his books.
[40] Young, p. viii.

have a developed intuitive understanding can ever know.

During one of her visits as she sat quietly watching Gibran alternately pacing the floor one moment, then walking to his desk to write, she walked to the desk, seated herself, and picked up the pencil ready to record the next thought. Gibran was taken unawares and immediately disapproved. However, in a short time his reluctance changed to consent. From this close relationship, Barbara Young was able to gather and to record various concepts and characteristics of Gibran.

There was another with whom Gibran shared an intimate friendship and to whom he could speak somewhat of his aloneness and his alienation. She was May Ziadeh, an eminent Lebanese writer who lived in Cairo, Egypt. She and Gibran never met personally, yet they developed and nourished a literary and intimate relationship through the many letters they wrote one another. They exchanged for criticism and comment books which each had written. May Ziadeh served as an outlet for the poet's pent-up passions and aspirations. He could write to her of his constant vacillation between a state of "acceptable" health and of soul-crushing illness. Once he wrote that pain "is an unseen and powerful hand that breaks the skin of the stone in order to extract the pulp."[41] Sometimes in resignation to his pain he would write:

> I have pleasure in being ill. This pleasure differs with its effect from other pleasure. I have found a sort of tranquility that makes me love illness. The sick man is safe from people's strife, demands, dates and appointments, excess of talking and ringing of telephones. . . I have found that I am closer to abstract things in my sickness than in health. When I lay my head and close my eyes and lose myself to the world,

[41] *Kahlil Gibran: A Self-Portrait*, p. 94.

*I find myself flying like a bird over serene valleys and
forests, wrapped in a gentle veil. I see myself close to
those whom my heart has loved, calling and talking
to them, but without anger and with the same feelings
they feel and the same thoughts they think. They lay
their hands now and then upon my forehead to bless
me.*[42]

In his extreme physical suffering, Gibran turned to the
power of the imagination to lessen his pain. However, imagination was not sufficient of itself; Gibran still felt the
desperate need for someone to share his life with him. In a
letter to May Ziadeh in 1930, one year before his death,
Gibran wrote:

*I am in no need for the doctors and their remedies,
nor for rest and silence. I am in dire need for one who
will relieve me of my burden. I am in need of a spiritual remedy—for a helpful hand to alleviate my con-
gested spirit. I am in need of a strong wind that will
fell my fruits and my leaves. . . I am, May, a small
volcano whose opening has been closed.*[43]

Gibran never found a mate to alleviate his feeling of
loneliness. Many women knew Gibran and loved him with
warmth and affection, and asked nothing of him in return.
There were others who thought themselves skillful in
deceiving him. The poet said,

*I am grateful for all love and affection. But they all
think I am much better than I am. They love the poet
and the painter, and would possess a bit of him. But
myself they do not see or know or love.*[44]

Once Gibran was asked why he did not marry.

[42] *Ibid.*, p. 84.
[43] *Ibid.*, p. 91.
[44] Young, p. 129.

"If I had a wife, and if I were painting or making poems, I should simply forget her existence for days at a time. And you know very well no loving woman would put up with such a husband very long."

. . . "But have you ever been in love?"

The change in his face was like lightning. He rose and stood, and when he spoke his voice was shaken with anger for the impertinence of the guest whom he was entertaining. Controlling himself with difficulty he said, "I will tell you a thing you may not know. The most highly sexed beings upon the planet are the creators, and poets, sculptors, painters, musicians and so it has been from the beginning. And among them sex is a beautiful exalted gift. Sex is always beautiful, and it is always shy."

. . . Then with another change of countenance and a look of pity for ignorance toward the questioner, who was, of course, a woman, he said, "As for myself, I do not know what in this world is not sex, do you? Only the little stones in the riverbed, perhaps, and the blown sands upon the shores of the great seas."[45]

After the departure of his friends, Gibran became silent, engrossed in thought. Then he said, "Silence is one of the mysteries of love."[46]

Mikhail Naimy, Gibran's biographer, tells of a young woman, unnamed, who met the poet in the last year of his life. Gibran asked for the second time, "Will you walk the road with me?" But it was too late, for in a few months that road came suddenly to an end.

As Gibran became better known in his adopted country, he met many whose behavior reminded him of that of

[45] *Ibid.*, pp. 129-130.
[46] *Ibid.*

his own people. Their thoughts, too, were as petrified as the thoughts of some in Lebanon. He said,

How often I talked with Harvard professors, yet felt as if I were talking to a professor from Al-Azhar![47] How often I have conversed with some Bostonian ladies and heard them say things I used to hear from simple and ignorant old women in Syria! Life is one, Mikhail; it manifests itself in the villages of Lebanon as in Boston, New York, and San Francisco.[48]

It pained Gibran to see America swing too swiftly to machinery and abandon her heritage of old world handicraft. He felt

something of vast value was being lost through the close and constant contact of men with machines, by way of the standardization that descended upon this country like a plague. "One of our lovely almost forgotten words is handmade," he said.[49]

Also America was becoming intoxicated with its many gadgets; it had the disease of faster-and-bigger. Gibran said,

"You [America] have wandered off from the road that your great, good men have travelled. But there is an Angel that is mindful of these United States—a very mighty and stubborn Angel. He is working to make you throw away two words—cleverness and publicity. These words are a stench in the nostrils of all angels and all gods. And remember this, he will not fail. This country will go back to the road, the road of Jefferson and Franklin, of Emerson and Whitman, and of Abraham Lincoln, the blessed."

[47] Al-Azhar is located in Cairo, Egypt. It is the oldest Moslem theological institution, and is known for its fanatical conservatism.
[48] Naimy, p. 241.
[49] Young, p. 133.

And on another day, still with a heart aching, and yet believing in the country of his adoption he said, "Perhaps the world is a sky-garden with races and civilizations for its blossoms. Some flourish well, from others the petals fall away. Here one is withered, and beside it there is left but an empty stalk to remind us of a great red-hearted bloom. Now on this rosebush, perhaps America is the bud just pressing to its sheath, ready to open; still hard, still green, and not yet fragrant, but vigorous and full of life."[50]

America became Gibran's home for all but twenty years of his life. Many were the times that he tired of the pace of cosmopolitan life and longed to return to the tranquility of Cedar Mountain and Lebanon. However, Gibran could never bring himself to leave his adopted country. Perhaps, even though Gibran criticized America, he loved her too. More and more Americans began to know and to love this poet and his little black books. "A lecture bureau offered to take him on a reading tour."[51] People wrote to him or called him expressing their admiration and appreciation for his books. The Queen of Rumania wrote to a friend in New York, thanking her for a gift copy of The Prophet, and requesting her to give her best regards to the author. Newspaper and magazine reviews were in the main complimentary.[52]

During the last years of Gibran's life, his countrymen endeavored to persuade him to return to Lebanon and become their leader in order to help the Lebanese solve their many problems. Gibran knew that such a move would be a mistake.

[50] Ibid., pp. 134-135.
[51] Naimy, p. 216.
[52] A thorough presentation of these reviews is given in a Master's thesis written by Martha Jean Ross, "The Writing of Kahlil Gibran" (Austin: University of Texas, 1948).

I am not that solution. I myself am a problem. If I went to Lebanon and took the little black book (The Prophet), and said, "Come let us live in this light," their enthusiasm for me would immediately evaporate. I am not a politician, and I would not be a politician.[53]

To his many young countrymen in America he wrote a message titled *To Young Americans of Syrian Origin*. It may serve as a loving admonition to young Americans whatever their origin may be. Gibran wrote:

I believe in you, and I believe in your destiny.

I believe that you are contributors to this new civilization.

I believe that you have inherited from your forefathers an ancient dream, a song, a prophecy, which you can proudly lay as a gift of gratitude upon the lap of America.

I believe that you can say to the founders of this great nation, "Here I am, a youth, a young tree whose roots were plucked from the hills of Lebanon, yet I am deeply rooted here, and I would be fruitful."

And I believe that you can say to Abraham Lincoln, the blessed, "Jesus of Nazareth touched your lips when you spoke, and guided your hand when you wrote; and I shall uphold all that you have said and all that you have written."

I believe that even as your fathers came to this land to produce riches, you were born to produce riches by intelligence and labor.

I believe that it is in you to be good citizens.

And what is it to be a good citizen?

It is to acknowledge the other person's rights before asserting your own, but always to be conscious of your own.

[53] Young, p. 125.

It is to be free in word and deed, but it is also to
know that your freedom is subject to the other person's
freedom.

It is to produce by labor and only by labor, and to
spend less than you have produced that your children
may not be dependent upon the state for support when
you are no more.

It is to stand before the towers of New York and
Washington, Chicago and San Francisco saying in your
hearts, "I am the descendant of a people that builded
Damascus and Byblos, and Tyre and Sidon and Antioch, and I am here to build with you, and with a will."

It is to be proud of being an American, but it is also
to be proud that your fathers and mothers came from
a land upon which God laid His gracious hand and
raised His messengers.

Young Americans of Syrian origin, I believe in you.[54]

In this message Gibran combines the ideal world of
thought with the practical world of activity. Significantly,
he stresses his faith in the young people's ability to achieve
a productive life. He reminds them of their proud heritage,
only to urge them to great deeds. He acknowledges the
opportunities existing in variegated America and he asks
them not only to receive but also to give. Most of all he
reiterates over and over again, "I believe that you can."
Gibran believed in youth and in their ability to fashion for
themselves a useful and a beautiful life. The affirmation of
life in its multiplicity of forms was first to be known, then
to be acted upon. Life then is the participation in the
handicraft of the Infinite, the "Great Sea which is called
God."[55]

[54] *Ibid.*, pp. 136-137.
[55] *Ibid.*, p. 147.

Gibran died the first Friday after Easter, April 10, 1931. His death was a great shock to his people. Too soon was their *habibi* (beloved) taken. The Arabic people are not ashamed to express their feelings of pain or sorrow, for their culture allows them outbursts of emotional behavior.[56]

Barbara Young describes the reactions of the people attending the little Church of Our Lady of the Cedars in Boston.

> An endless stream of sorrowing humanity passed silently before the quiet form of their habibi, and the word was murmured between sobs, by young and old. Many of these mourners were people from his own country. . . Many a one dropped upon his knees and sobbed aloud, and the young guard of honor, with tears overflowing, stood immovable. . .
>
> Never to be forgotten was the wonder of it, the complete abandonment of anguish of these people, the beauty of their faces, a tragic beauty, and the words they spoke to me about this loving man lying silent before them.
>
> . . . Outside were hundreds who could not gain admission. And when the service was over, we who passed out between the waiting crowds saw a sight seldom seen in any Western city. Hundreds of people dropped on their knees, on the sidewalks, in the street, and there was a sound of low, hardly controlled weeping that was almost unearthly in its rhythm.[57]

This united tribute to Kahlil Gibran evidenced the love and loss his countrymen felt for him. They felt a unified sense of having lost a part of themselves in the departure of a man who had put into words their deepest

[56] Hamady, *op. cit.*, p. 46.
[57] Young, pp. 152-153.

longings, their silent needs. Gibran himself had felt most deeply these silent longings to the very end of his life. The stranger was indeed not a stranger. Whether Gibran perceived this fact or not we do not know, but in a certain sense it is so. For he too had suffered, had lost, and had loved. He was one of them. Truly through his words and deeds, Gibran now is one of us.

> In the great tower of the Shove Memorial Chapel at Colorado College is a set of Westminister chimes cast at Croyden, England, with a master bell weighing six tons, which will strike the hours. And upon the bell are graven the words,
>
> YESTERDAY IS BUT TODAY'S MEMORY,
> AND TOMORROW IS TODAY'S DREAM.
>   KAHLIL GIBRAN[58]

Seven years after Gibran's death, G. W. Russell declared the outstanding achievement of Gibran. Russell said, "I do not think the East has spoken with so beautiful a voice since the *Gitanjali* of Rabindranath Tagore as in *The Prophet* of Kahlil Gibran."[59] Russell praises the beauty of Gibran's thought, "which exercises a deeper enchantment than the beauty of form."[60] The question is asked by Russell,

> I wonder has the East many more poets to reveal to us? If Europe is to have a new renaissance comparable to that which came from the wedding of Christianity with the Greek and Latin culture it must, I think, come from a second wedding of Christianity with the culture of the East. Our own words to each other

[58] *Ibid.*, p. 183.
[59] G. W. Russell, *Kahlil Gibran, Living Torch* (New York: Macmillan, 1938), p. 168.
[60] *Ibid.*

bring us no surprise. It is only when a voice comes from India or China or Arabia that we get the thrill of strangeness from the beauty, and we feel that it might inspire another of the great cultural passions of humanity.[61]

In 1956 the Institute of Islamic studies met at the Sorbonne in Paris to discuss contemporary Lebanese poetry.[62] Jean Lecerf tells of hearing the Rector of the Lebanese University, Fouad Ephrem Boustany, extol the living works of Kahlil Gibran the great poet, novelist, essayist, dramatic author, and above all philosopher and painter. Jean Lecerf credits Gibran's emigration to America and his contact with the prose poems of Friedrich Nietzsche as factors which influenced Gibran in creating a new Arabic genre. Lecerf says the influence of Nietzsche in Gibran's works is evidenced in the avenging and passionate tone of his essays. Gibran is described as cultivating a style of his own in the Arab world which has something of

> Biblical imitation, of the Psalms of David, of the Song of Songs of Solomon, of the Book of Job, of the Lamentations of Jeremiah, of the visions of Isaiah, as well as the exhortations of the Galilean, a style in which no author of the Arabic or English language had preceded him and which in Europe had only been practiced by Freidrich Nietzsche.[63]

Lecerf states that the writing of prose poems was the fashion in 1910, and that the attempts of the various authors could not be brought into perfect unity. There are

[61] *Ibid.*, p. 169.
[62] Jean Lecerf, "Djabran Kahlil Djabran et les origines de la prose poetique moderne," trans. Mildred Hansen, *Orient*, No. 3 (1957).
[63] *Ibid.*, p. 11. This quotation is a translation by Jean Lecerf from the German of Carl Brockelman, who dedicates eleven pages to Gibran in his book *The Literary History of the Arabs*.

two principle traits of the prose poem genre. The first was
the reaction against the classical rhymed prose. "The essential elements of the prose poem consist in the parallelism,
and its reinforcement by a repetition which can sometimes
go into a sort of refrain."[64] The second trait is the imitation
of the sacred texts. In the other Arabic authors, for example
Amin Raihani, it is an unconscious imitation of the Koran,
but in Gibran it is an avowed imitation of Biblical style.
Raihani's prose, like the verse of the Koran, is difficult to
translate whereas

> the subtile harmonies of the rhyme-free fragments
> from the writings of Gibran are definitely preserved in
> translation, in the same way the Biblical style repre-
> sented, since Saint Jerome, for majority of Christians a
> style of translations of which the English language
> even possessed an "authorized version."[65]

Jean Lecerf remarks that the Biblical references evident in Gibran's writings seem much less the result of
imitation of a model than of a conscious effort to realize
a sort of Nietzschean echo in his style. Gibran's effort goes
beyond the Koran itself, and the poet rediscovers still more
ancient sources of inspiration. Lecerf concludes

> Kahlil Gibran, lost child of the Arab nation, in his
> distant emigration may be found designed by destiny
> to take part in this new evolution of a poetic genre,
> the "prose."[66]

[64] Ibid., p. 12.
[65] Ibid., p. 13.
[66] Ibid., p. 14.

2

Gibran's Use of the Parable

THE WORD "PARABLE" is derived from the Greek
parabole, appearing in Latin as *parabola*. Its root meaning
is from the combination of *para*, beside, and *ballein*, to
throw. It means a placing beside or a comparison. Since the
comparison was done by means of speech, the idea of *speaking* moved through Italian and French to appear in English
as "parole" (one's word), "parlance" (one's manner of
speech), or even "parlor" (the speaking room). The concept that the parable is a comparison remains with the
word "parable" as it is used today.

Many figures of speech make comparisons to suggest
various meanings; however, not all of them are called parables. A metaphor is a short, compact, implied comparison.
Typically, the writer asserts that one thing is, in some
respects, another or that it acts like or has some of the
qualities of something else; for example "a *lyric poet* with
a *pipeline* to the simplest and strongest emotions," or a
"raging sea." A simile says specifically that one thing is like
another, using the word *like* or *as*, for example, "a cliff has
a beetling brow like a man who is frowning." When the

metaphor is extended so that every detail reveals some truth by its comparison, it is called an allegory, as Bunyan's *Pilgrims Progress* in which concrete characters, often with identifying tag-names, are personifications of abstract ideas. By definition the parable is a fictitious narrative or allegory of "events in human life or of a process in nature, by which some great spiritual truth is illustrated or enforced."[1] Moreover, the parable conceals truth as well as it reveals truth. Therefore, the parable must be approached with some previous insight in order to understand the moral and spiritual lesson it unfolds. At the same time, the parable is employed to stimulate inquiry for truth in the seeming contradictions of life experiences.

Upon being asked why he spoke to them in parables, Jesus said:

> For whosoever hath, to him shall be given, and he shall have more abundance: but whosoever hath not, from him shall be taken away even that he hath.
>
> Therefore speak I to them in parables: because they seeing see not; and hearing they hear not, neither do they understand.[2]

Gibran once said in a letter to Mikhail Naimy, "Do not endeavor to awaken those whose hearts God has put to sleep for some hidden reason."[3]

The parables of Gibran are here interpreted within the framework of five principles.[4] First, "since the parable is a developed comparison, its principal lesson is to be found

---

[1] William M. Taylor, *The Parables of Our Saviour* (New York: Doubleday Doran, 1929), p. 2. This definition is used because it succinctly expresses the various dictionary explanations.

[2] Matthew 13: 12, 13.

[3] *Kahlil Gibran: A Self-Portrait*, p. 61.

[4] The following five principles are taken from Francis L. Filas', *The Parables of Jesus* (New York: The Macmillan Company, 1959), pp. 2-3.

by presenting the narrative in the two terms of its comparison";[5] that is, the fictional narration and the spiritual reality or lesson.

The second principle to bear in mind is that every minute detail must not be given significance. There are secondary details which only function to enforce the image or illustration. They do not apply directly to the lesson of the parable.

In addition, notice should be given to the existence of literary details—the use of various expressions and words employed to render an emotional effect or elevated style. These expressions may be dropped without changing the imagery or the spiritual lesson of the parable.

Parables may describe certain life processes, but they are not designed to follow everyday reality in exact detail. Sometimes parables are purposely vague and indefinite. The emphasis is here placed on a *priori* knowledge of the reader which enables him to grasp the import of the parable.

A final consideration involves a word of caution. "Some parables end with an 'apparent' conclusion which should not be interpreted as part of the main lesson."[6] Only the logical lesson of the first illustration should be accepted, and the second or apparent short maxim should serve for further reflection.

The area of investigation specifically treated in the study which follows is an interpretation of Gibran's messages to man in society as they are revealed in his parables. His horizon and his social theories underwent change and clarification as his powers developed and as his experiences gave him maturity. Thus the method employed here is to present his ideas in an order paralleling his thought processes during his successive stages of developmental change.

[5] *Ibid.*
[6] *Ibid.*

There is one additional explanation that I find it necessary to make. I am cognizant of the fact that parables may
be interpreted differently in accordance with the propen-
sities of the reader. Therefore, the interpretations which
follow are explications of the spiritual lesson of Gibran's
parables; an attempt is made to indicate universal application, which is the application of the spiritual message to the
existing conditions of society perceived in the light of present day thnking and the present knowledge of the writer.

Thus, in the language of the parable, Gibran describes
the nature of the distances between man and man and suggests the means whereby these distances may be spanned.
"Know you not that there is no distance save that which the
soul does not span in fancy? And when the soul shall span
the distance, it becomes a rhythm in the soul."[7] It is precisely this rhythm within man's soul that Gibran's parables
attempt to reveal to man. Rhythm produces a kind of harmony that not only originates a joy in its beholder, but also
creates a state of being which draws men together in understanding. Much of man's spiritual awareness is dimmed by
men's prohibitive laws and limiting fears. Gibran's parables
delineate repeatedly the possibility that man's dreams or
fancy, which are man's ability to perceive the ideal or universal character of experience, can, rather than separate man
from man, create a communion or a sharing in the existent
spiritual essence of man. In this possibility lies man's only
hope of resolving the recurrent, useless conflicts in himself
and consequently in earthly experience, which collectively
is called civilization.

Gibran's parables portray first an awareness of existing
relations, of the possibility that these relations can be
changed, and finally, of the motivations and behavior neces-

[7] Kahlil Gibran, *The Garden of the Prophet* (New York: Alfred A.
Knopf, 1933), p. 21.

sary for change. The early parables, beginning with *The Madman*, are primarily descriptive observations of the ways of men. At times, the tone is quite bitter and ironic. The tone in the later parables, however, becomes melancholy, the irony disappears, and in its place are kindly parables that impart the spiritual lesson. The discussions of the parables follow Gibran's development from the early denouncing tone inherent in *The Madman* to the transitional phase of *The Forerunner*, and finally, to the understanding of himself and his relationship with others in *The Wanderer*.

The question may be asked, "Why the use of parables by Gibran?" Obviously this question cannot be answered conclusively; however, there are several significant facts which should be recognized. The parable is a literary form peculiar to the East. Gibran, born of Eastern heritage, spent eighteen years of his life in the East. He received his academic training at Al-Madrasat in Lebanon where he also underwent intensified religious instruction. It can be assumed that he became familiar with the original language of the Aramaic parable, the technique employed, and its unique and effective manner of portraying a spiritual truth. The parabolical method of teaching as employed by Jesus was a veiled expedient that safely proclaimed His intended message. To those who were familiar with His teachings, the parable served to increase their knowledge and perception of truth. Those who did not know or who did not wish to know of His purpose could neither condemn nor receive the spiritual message. The parables of Jesus were not easily understood in His day, for there were several repetitions as, for example, the many stories which begin with "The Kingdom of God is like." Gibran said, "Few of us are able to add fact to different fact and make a truth thereof."[8]

[8] Kahlil Gibran, *The Wanderer* (New York: Alfred A. Knopf, 1932), p. 55.

Gibran, therefore, attempts the difficult task of transferring into the English language the Aramaic parable with its conceptual unity in diversity.

Goethe recognized the ability of the Arab to see identity-within-difference[9] when he said:

> All things which man expresses fully and naturally are life-relations; now the Arab is as intimately connected with camel and horse as is body and soul; nothing can happen to him which does not at the same time affect these creatures and vitally connect their existence and their activity with his own. . . If we proceed to consider everything else visible: mountains and desert, cliff and plain, trees, herbs, flowers, rivers and sea and the starry heavens, we find that to the Oriental, ALL THINGS SUGGEST ALL THINGS, so that, accustomed to connect the most remote things together, he does not hesitate to derive contrary things from one another by very slight changes in letters and syllables. Here we see that language is already productive in and of itself, and indeed, in so far as it comes to meet thought, is eloquent and, in so far as it coincides with the imagination, is poetic. [EMPHASIS MINE.][10]

Goethe's observations of the Arab and his language have been presented here to explain in part Gibran's use of word images unfamiliar to the Western mind. It should be recognized as a natural effect of his Arabic heritage that "to the Oriental, all things suggest all things."[11] The critic Elijah Jordan has generalized this phenomenon by declaring

[9] This term is borrowed from E. Jordan in his book *Essays in Criticism* (Chicago: University of Chicago Press, 1953), p. 215.

[10] Quoted by Ernst Robert Curtius, *European Literature and the Latin Middle Ages*, Willard A. Trask, translator from the German (New York: Pantheon Books, 1953), p. 303.

[11] *Ibid.*

that "it is questionable if there are any 'discordant qualities' in the artist's world." Among writers whose native languages were not originally English, Gibran's writings in the English language served to set his name, along with that of Joseph Conrad, as one of the six men writing the most notable contemporary English. This recognition pleased Gibran, but he realized that he was a guest to the language and must treat it with deference. He said, "I may not take the liberties which its own sons may take."[12]

Another observation made by an Arabist who studied the ancient Arabic poets, as Gibran must have, comments on their intensity of feeling and their ability to express that feeling in highly poetic words.

> *They were natural poets . . . impulsive children of the desert, whose passions had free scope for good and evil; who were capable of the most intense affection, and of the most bitter hatred; whose strong feelings found vent in flowing verse.*[13]

THE MASKS

Gibran gave vent to passionate outpourings in his first English book, *The Madman.*[14] The book opens with the story of a man who became a madman. It seems that the man awoke one morning to find all of his masks were gone. Frightened, unprotected by masks, he ran into the streets shouting and cursing the thieves who stole his masks. The people laughed at him, and one boy who was standing on a housetop cried, "He is a madman."[15] When the madman

[12] Kahlil Gibran, *Prose Poems*, trans. Andrew Grareeb (New York: Alfred A. Knopf, 1934), p. vii.

[13] W. A. Clouston, (ed.), "Introduction," *Arabian Poetry*, (Glasgow: M'Laren and Sons, 1881), p. xxxvi.

[14] Kahlil Gibran, *The Madman* (New York: Alfred A. Knopf, 1918).

[15] *The Madman*, p. 7.

looked up to see him, the sun kissed his naked face and inflamed his soul with love for the sun, so that he no longer wanted his masks. Then he blessed the thieves who stole his masks, and became a madman. In his madness, he discovered a freedom which was in part loneliness, and in part safety derived from being misunderstood. "For those who understand us enslave something in us."[16]

It is said that in his youth, Gibran "conceived the universe as perfect and devoid of evil."[17] Men were just and wise in their relations with one another. Once he discovered that justice is capable of being corrupted and that superstitions and evil customs prevail, he became disillusioned and embittered. He took upon himself the task of exposing the evil deeds of men. Like the ancient poet Di'bil, he too believed that "men were most influenced by the fear that their defects be broadcast."[18] Moreover, these fears create untold suffering, even crucifixion and this, too, must be revealed.

CRUCIFIXION

"Crucified"[19] is the parable of a man who sought to be crucified. The people turned away from him for fear of being accused of his murder. The man insisted, telling them that only by crucifying madmen would they be exalted. Wanting to be exalted, they crucified him. This turn of events satisfied the madman for he said:

And when I was hanged between earth and heaven they lifted up their heads to see me. And they were exalted, for their heads had never before been lifted.[20]

[16] *Ibid.*, p. 8.
[17] Kahlil Gibran, *Thoughts and Meditations*, Anthony R. Ferris, trans. (New York: The Citadel Press, 1960), p. 7.
[18] Leon Zolondek, *Di'bil b.'Ali, The Life and Writing of an Early Abbasid Poet* (Kentucky: University of Kentucky Press, 1961), p. 7.
[19] *The Madman*, p. 57.
[20] *Ibid.*

Still they did not understand. Looking up at his crucified figure, they began to question him. What did he wish
to atone for? In what cause did he sacrifice himself? Was
this a price he wished to pay for glory? Finally, one man
called out,

> "Behold how he smiles! Can such pain be forgiven?"
> And I answered them all and said:
> "Remember only that I smiled. I do not atone—
> nor sacrifice—nor wish for glory and I have nothing to
> forgive. I thirsted—and I besought you to give me my
> blood to drink. For what is there can quench a mad-
> man's thirst but his own blood? I was dumb—and I
> asked wounds of you for mouths. I was imprisoned in
> your days and nights—and I sought a door into larger
> days and nights.
>
> And now I go—as others already crucified have
> gone. And think not we are weary of crucifixion. For
> we must be crucified by larger and yet larger men,
> between greater earths and greater heavens."[21]

This is a parable of man's search for spiritual revelation
and spiritual fulfillment unmindful of the physical sacrifice
involved. The act of crucifixion is familiar to most people
in all ages. Crucifixion has been accepted in one form or
another by idealistic men throughout recorded history.
Socrates' drinking of the hemlock and Jesus' acquiesence to
crucifixion are two well known examples. The idealistic man
embraces the extreme act of self-sacrifice for his idea of the
good and the right. Although other men may consider him
mad, he does not falter. His silent need demands expression and urges him on beyond self to a Universal Self of
Principle. In this manner he frees his spirit from a narrow,
limited view of the world to a vaster unfettered vision of
the world that embraces all men in all worlds.

[21] Ibid., p. 58.

Literary expressions such as "I thirsted—and I besought you to give me my blood to drink," and "I was dumb—and I asked wounds for mouths," only serve to deepen the emotional impact and to enforce the macabre image of the crucifixion. They do not detract from the lesson of the parable.

The lesson of Gibran's parable is twofold. First, to know life and to plumb its depths for meaning, one must suffer. "The steed swiftest to carry you to perfection is suffering,"[22] said Meister Eckhart, great German medieval monk. Suffering is encountered in the struggle for freedom from man's imprisonment in man's blind limiting laws. The second spiritual lesson touched by the parable has to do with the cheerful acceptance of pain. The madman felt no guilt; therefore he had nothing for which to atone. He sought no glory, no fame. He only sought truth through self-revelation, and in that very quest lay his joy. He said, "Remember only that I smiled."

The concluding paragraph of Gibran's parable is an added reflection on mankind in general. His crucifixion is a continuum. Men before him have been crucified and men after him will continue to be crucified. Therefore, his crucifixion comes not as a surprise but as a necessary experience in man's journey toward spiritual awareness.

In an earlier parable,[23] written when Gibran was scarcely twenty years old, crucifixion is described in still another aspect. In an open field stood a poet. By the side of a flowing stream, he saw a perfectly built bird cage. Inside the cage lay a dead bird. Beside the bird's body lay two empty basins. The caged bird had died of thirst and

[22] Raymond B. Blakney, trans., Meister Eckhart (New York: Harper and Brothers, 1957), p. 90.
[23] Kahlil Gibran, "Vision," Tears and Laughter, Anthony R. Ferris, trans. (New York: The Philosophical Library, 1949), p. 58.

hunger in the midst of a rich field and near a flowing stream.

Suddenly, before the poet's eyes the cage becomes a human skeleton and the dead bird a man's heart, wounded and bleeding. "A voice comes from the wound saying, 'I am the human heart, prisoner of substance and victim of earthly laws.' "[24] The voice from the wound continues to lament his imprisonment, his terrible neglect by humanity, and the binding chains of earthly authority amid the free bounty of God's field and God's beautiful Creation.

All these words the poet heard as he gazed at the bleeding heart until his eyes became so misty he could not see, and his crying soul could bear no more.

The lesson of this Gibranic parable is one of awareness of suffering that is inflicted by man's inhumanity to man. Man builds artificial walls to bind man to earthly authority, yet that very authority neglects him in his bondage, and finally causes his death in the midst of potential freedom and plenty.

In a later work, Gibran looks with compassion on the errors and foibles of men. To those who seek to pave the way to a better life, he gives assurance even in adversity.

> To be robbed, cheated, deceived, ay, misled and trapped and then mocked, yet with it all to look down from the height of your larger self and smile . . . knowing that all these deemed wrongdoers are your brothers in need . . .
>
> I would have you each and every one partners to the purpose of every man, for only so shall you hope to obtain your own good purpose.[25]

[24] *Ibid.*, p. 59.
[25] Kahlil Gibran, *The Garden of the Prophet* (New York: Alfred A. Knopf, 1933), pp. 48-49.

Thus self-revelation, though it embodies suffering and pain, because of its nature eliminates all superficialities, reaches the core of man, and discovers a humility and a sympathy toward all of mankind. So-called wrongdoers are simply brothers in need. "No man is an island entire of itself,"[26] and every man is a partner to the purpose of every other man. In this manner, man can hope to obtain his own good purpose.

AUTHORITY

Concern over the misuse of authority compelled Gibran to write many scorching expository articles. From early childhood, Gibran rebelled at imposed authority. His rebellion took various forms throughout his life. Gibran progressed from direct condemnation of specific events and practices already noted in the previous chapter, to parables of denunciation, and at last in his later work, to a concept of action whereby the governed may recognize their own power to govern.

The parable of "The Wise King"[27] portrays a "wise" king who yielded to the superstitious beliefs of his people rather than lose his authority over them. In the beginning, the narrative describes the king of Wirani as mighty and wise. He was loved for his wisdom and feared for his might. Now in the center of the city was a well the waters of which were ever cool and crystalline. The well provided water for the entire populace and for the king and his court. "One night when all were asleep, a witch entered the city, and poured seven drops of strange liquid into the well, and

----

[26] John Donne, "xvii. Meditation," *Seventeenth-Century Prose and Poetry*, Robert P. Tristram Coffin and Alexander M. Witherspoon, eds. (New York: Harcourt, Brace, 1946), p. 68.
[27] *The Madman*, p. 27.

said, 'From this hour he who drinks this water shall become mad.' "[28]

The next day all the people drank from the well except the king and his lord chamberlain. The people at once became mad. They began to gather together and to whisper to one another, "The king is mad. Our king and his lord chamberlain have lost their reason. Surely we cannot be ruled by a mad king. We must dethrone him."[29]

When the king heard of these rumors, he immediately called for a golden goblet and commanded that it be filled from the waters of the well. This command was performed. The king drank deeply and he gave also to his lord chamberlain to drink. His action satisfied the people. They rejoiced for now their king had regained his reason.

The title of this parable is an ironic misnomer. The king had ruled with the strength of wisdom. However, when the people's minds were poisoned by the magic actions of the witch, who represents evil and superstition, they mistook wisdom for madness. In their state of ignorance, they turned against their wise king. The king, to retain his authority over them, satisfied them by conforming to their desires and becoming like them.

The parable concludes with the declaration that now the people rejoiced. For now, in a much different manner, the "wise" king again became the reflection of the people.

The literary symbols "witch" and "seven drops of strange liquid" are of course fictional, but they do not detract from the meaning of the analogy. The lesson is still clear when attention is given to the reactions of the king to his subjects.

Two years later, Gibran wrote the parable of "The

[28] Ibid.
[29] Ibid., p. 28.

Lion's Daughter."[30] The parable concerns a sleeping queen, her four slaves, and her cat. While the queen sleeps, the slaves confess their hatred and fear of the queen. The cat, whose silent thoughts are italicized in the parable, answers and comments on the conversations of the slaves and on the conditions of slavery.

The parable opens as the slaves have just stopped fanning the queen, who has fallen asleep on her throne. The first slave bursts out in bitterness, saying that the old woman is ugly, that her mouth droops, and that her snores sound as if the devil himself were choking her. The cat purrs her comment that the old queen is not half as ugly in her sleep as they are in their open wide-awake slavery.

The second slave points to the deep wrinkles on the old queen's face and attributes them to the tenseness of an evil dream. The cat silently wishes that the slaves themselves might sleep and dream of freedom.

The third slave remarks that the old queen is probably seeing in her sleep a procession of all those she has slain. To this remark, the cat agrees and says that the procession is composed of the slaves' forefathers and their descendants.

The fourth slave voices her weariness at having to stand continuously and fan the old queen. The cat purrs, "You shall be fanning to all eternity; for as it is on earth so it is in heaven."[31]

At that moment, the old queen nods her head and her crown falls to the floor. One slave cries that it is a bad omen. The cat answers, "The bad omen of one is the good omen of another."[32]

The second slave says fearfully that if the queen should

[30] Kahlil Gibran, The Forerunner (New York: Alfred A. Knopf, 1920), p. 22.
[31] Ibid., p. 23.
[32] Ibid.

awaken and find her crown had fallen, she would slay them. Here, the cat's answer is that they are slain every day and they do not know it.

The third slave agrees with the second slave that they might be slain and that their deaths would be called a sacrifice to the gods. The cat's answer is that only the weak are sacrificed to the gods.

The fourth slave quiets the others, picks up the crown, and replaces it on the head of the queen. The cat purrs that only a slave restores a crown that has fallen.

And after a while the old queen woke, and she looked about her and yawned. Then she said, "Methought I dreamed, and I saw four caterpillars chased by a scorpion around the trunk of an ancient oak tree. I like not my dream."

Then she closed her eyes and went to sleep again. And she snored. And the four slaves went on fanning her.

And the cat purred, "Fan on, fan on, stupids. You fan but the fire that consumes you."[33]

This Gibranic parable verbalizes condemnatory and subservient thoughts that exist in the minds of those who are slaves or who are compelled by various means to be in bondage to others. The slaves are four in number, physically stronger than one weak, old, sleeping queen. But fear of authority, which the queen represents, keeps them powerlessly subjugated in her service. They simply argue about their condition. Yet they do not attempt to change it. That they could change their situation never enters their minds.

It is the cat, appropriately called the lion's daughter, who declares the lesson of the parable. If the slaves could only dream of freedom, that is, become aware of freedom in

[33] *Ibid.*, pp. 24-25.

imagination or thought, they would suddenly realize that
freedom exists. And it could exist for them.

The slaves have been servants for many years; they are
weary of being held in bondage, yet they are not aware that
their fears have chained them into a state of inaction. The
accident of the fallen crown should have shown them the
vulnerability of authority. Instead, they consider it a bad
omen, a further proof of their superstitious beliefs, and
quickly replace the crown on the head of the sleeping
queen.

The queen's dream is analogous to the relationship
existing between her and her slaves. Although the queen
declares her dislike for the dream, she nevertheless discards
it from her mind and placidly resumes sleeping.

Neither the queen nor the slaves attempt to change
the situation. She is acquiescent in her role of authority as
the slaves are subservient to that authority. They grumble
and rumble, chafing in their bondage, fanning the very fire
that consumes them.

A proper relationship between a ruler and those who
are ruled is delineated in Gibran's parable "The King."[34]
It appears that one day the people of the kingdom of Sadik
gathered in front of the palace shouting rebellion against
their king. The king, dressed in his royal robe, came down
the steps carrying his crown in one hand and his sceptre in
the other. His stately appearance silenced the people. He
said:

> My friends, who are no longer my subjects, here I
> yield my crown and sceptre unto you. I would be one
> of you. I am only one man, but as a man I would work
> together with you that our lot may be made better.
> There is no need for a king. Let us go therefore to the

[34] The Wanderer, p. 22.

fields and the vineyards and labor hand with hand. Only you must tell me to what field or vineyard I should go. All of you now are king.[35]

The king's action took the people by surprise, for they had blamed the king for their discontent. And here the king was giving up his symbols of authority to become one of them. They returned to their homes; and the king accompanied one of them to a field.

The conditions in the kingdom remained the same, and the people were still discontented. They began to search for their king. He was found laboring in the field. They brought him back to the palace, returned his crown and sceptre to him, and proclaimed him their king. Then they requested that he rule them with strength and justice.

Now the people had one to whom they could come with their misfortunes. This time they did not come to blame him but to tell him of specific people who mistreated them. There was a baron who was cruel to them. The baron was brought before the king. The king said to the baron, "The life of one man is as weighty in the scales of God as the life of another."[36] Because the baron did not treat his workers justly, he was banished from the kingdom.

The next day, another group came to the king to inform him of the cruelty of a countess. She, too, was brought before the king, who informed her, "Those who till our fields and care for our vineyards are nobler than we who eat the bread they prepare and drink the wine of their wine-press."[37] So the countess was banished from the kingdom.

Then the people came to the king to complain of a bishop who made them carry stones and hew them for the

[35] Ibid.
[36] Ibid., p. 24.
[37] Ibid.

cathedral, yet he gave them nothing for their labor. More-over, the bishop possessed much gold and silver. The king requested the bishop to come before him. The king said to him, "That cross you wear upon your bosom should mean giving life unto life. But you have taken life from life and given none."[38] The bishop, also, was banished from the kingdom.

As it happened, on a certain day the people gathered again before the palace and called for their king. The king appeared prepared to relinquish his crown and sceptre. The people refused to accept them. Instead, they declared their thanks giving to him for ridding the land of vipers and wolves.

Then the king said, "Not I, not I. You yourself are king. When you deemed me weak and a misruler, you yourself were weak and misruling. And now the land fares well because it is in your will. I am but a thought in the mind of you all, and I exist not save in your actions. There is no such thought as governor. Only the governed exist to govern themselves."

And the king re-entered his tower with his crown and sceptre. And the elders and the youths went their various ways and they were content.

And each and every one thought of himself as king with a crown in one hand and a sceptre in the other.[39]

Gibran's message in this final parable on authority is one of cooperative responsibility between the ruler and the people. One reflects the actions of the other. The king establishes the necessary relationship between them when he says, "I am but a thought in the mind of you all, and I exist not save in your actions." When the people began

[38] *Ibid.*, p. 25.
[39] *Ibid.*, p. 26.

to act in accordance with this understanding, an improvement in their situation became a natural consequence. They brought to the king's attention certain unjust practices, represented by the baron, the countess, and the bishop, and these were eliminated.

In this parable the king acts as a catalyst, creating certain life situations which stimulate certain actions on the part of the people. This new spirit of action is directed at achieving proper conditions in the kingdom. The "of the people, by the people, and for the people" declaration becomes in Gibran's parable "the governed exist to govern themselves."

THE POET

Early in his career Gibran was asked to appear before The Poetry Society to read from his poems. Gibran read to them his prose poem "Night and the Madman."[40] "He came out of the meeting boiling with anger and resentment, for the audience received him and his piece with coldness that amounted to hissing mockery."[41] Undaunted as he was when his book *Spirits Rebellious* was publicly burned,

[40] In this poem the madman compares himself with the night. The madman says that he is like the night dark and naked, silent and deep, wild and terrible, cruel and awful, joyous and glad, patient and passionate, and mighty and high. He gives his reasons for each comparison. The night, meanwhile, answers negatively giving his reasons why the madman is not like him. The poem ends with the madman's assertion, "Yea, we are twin brothers, O, Night; for thou revealest space and I reveal my soul." In other words, the night reveals the actions that take place in space while the madman reveals the actions that take place in his thoughts or soul. The word images used in the comparisons were apparently unfamiliar and, to say the least, unusual for that particular poetry audience of perhaps forty years ago. They were obviously shocked into repulsion. The poem is from *The Madman*, page 49.

[41] Mikhail Naimy, *Kahlil Gibran: A Biography* (New York: The Philosophical Library, 1950), p. 140.

Gibran at once composed a passionate poem titled "Defeat":[42]

Defeat, my Defeat, my deathless courage,
You and I shall laugh together with the storm,
And together we shall dig graves for all that die in us,
And we shall stand in the sun with a will,
And we shall be dangerous.[43]

A few months later, in a letter to Naimy, Gibran informed him of readings he had given from The Madman, The Forerunner, and The Prophet before an audience who appreciated "this kind of thinking and this style of writing."[44]

Gibran wrote prolifically concerning the poet and his works. At times, Gibran wrote with a tinge of humor. One of his lighter parables, "Poets,"[45] has to do with four poets sitting around a bowl of wine placed on a table. The first poet, speaking as if he were in a daze, says that with his third eye he sees the fragrance of the wine "hovering in space like a cloud of birds in an enchanted forest."[46]

In the same manner, the second poet refers to his inner ear, with which he can hear mist-birds singing. "And the melody holds my heart as the white rose imprisons the bee within her petals."[47] Still referring to imaginary senses,

[42] The Madman, p. 46.
[43] The Madman, pp. 47-48. This the last stanza of a five-stanza poem. "Defeat" was included in its entirety in a choreographic mime entitled Office Drawn from The Rhythms of Kahlil Gibran, 1936. This mime was performed at St. Mark's in-the-Bouwerie, an Episcopal church in New York City. This information was received through the office of the assistant minister of the church, who directed me to the Andover-Harvard Theological Library, recipient of Dr. William Norman Guthrie's papers. Dr. Guthrie inaugurated the mime based on Gibran's works.
[44] Naimy, op. cit., p. 253.
[45] The Forerunner, p. 35.
[46] Ibid.
[47] Ibid.

the third poet closes his eyes and stretching his arms upward says, "I touch them with my hand. I feel their wings, like the breath of a sleeping fairy, brushing against my fingers."[48]

Whereupon the fourth poet rises, picks up the bowl of wine, and says:

"Alas, friends! I am too dull of sight and of hearing and of touch. I cannot see the fragrance of this wine, nor hear its song, nor feel the beating of its wings. I perceive but the wine itself. Now therefore must I drink it, that it may sharpen my senses and raise me to your blissful heights."

And putting the bowl to his lips, he drank the punch to the very last drop.

The three poets, with their mouths open, looked at him aghast, and there was a thirsty yet unlyrical hatred in their eyes.[49]

The lesson is quite clear. The drinking of the wine symbolizes the need for active participation in experience if one is to increase his knowledge and enjoyment of a thing. Words that merely describe passive thoughts, no matter how eloquent, must be based on actual experience to "sharpen the senses" and consequently to enable the senses to reach "blissful heights."

The concluding sentence exposes the feelings of the three poets clearly. The poets became angry at the poet who, unlike them, preferred to discover the reality of his senses rather than speculate gloriously about intangibles.

Another Gibranic parable, "The Two Poems,"[50] is given a setting many centuries ago. On a road to Athens, two poets meet and greet one another joyfully. One poet

48 Ibid.
49 Ibid., p. 36.
50 The Wanderer, p. 64.

asks the other poet if he has composed anything lately. The
other poet says with pride that he has written perhaps the
greatest poem yet written in Greek. "It is an invocation to
Zeus the Supreme."[51] Then he says that he wishes to read
it to the other poet. So they sit down in the shade of a
cypress tree, and the poet reads his poem. It is a long poem.
The other poet compliments him kindly on the poem and
tells him that it is indeed a great poem, that it will live
through the ages, and that because of it he shall be glorified.
Whereupon the first poet asks the other poet if he has
written a poem lately.

*And the other answered, "I have written but little.
Only eight lines in remembrance of a child playing in
a garden." And he recited the lines.*

The first poet said, "Not so bad; not so bad."

And they parted.

*And now after two thousand years the eight lines of
the one poet are read in every tongue, and are loved
and cherished.*

*And though the other poem has indeed come down
through the ages in libraries and in the cells of scholars,
and though it is remembered, it is neither loved nor
read.[52]*

The spiritual message can readily be deduced from the
words of the poet who wrote the simple short poem about
a child playing in a garden. The child represents life and
youth and wonder, symbols of growth and of nature. His
simple poem is known by all peoples of all languages and
it is loved and cherished. The other poet had written a great
poem, and it, too, has come down through the ages; but it
is housed in libraries and the cells of scholars. The poem

[51] *Ibid.*
[52] *Ibid.*, p. 65.

is a prayer to Zeus, who is a symbol of a thought crystallized, exalted, and glorified; Zeus is not a living movement in life. Gibran said of Greece:

> Greece borrowed her gods from Chaldea, Phoenicia, and Egypt. She borrowed every quality save that vision, that insight, that peculiar consciousness of what is deeper than depth and higher than height . . . She was capable of fashioning the naively formed jug and cup into golden vessels, but she never filled them with aught but liquid realism.
>
> To me the only mighty being in the Greek mythology is Prometheus, but let us not forget that the original fire-bringer is Chaldean and not Greek. The races of Western Asia knew him two thousand years before the Trojan expedition.
>
> . . . I love it [Greek art] for what it is, not for what it is not. I love the charm, the freshness, the loveliness, the physical glory of all things Grecian, but I cannot find in these the living God. I see only a shadow of His shadow.[53]

To Gibran "that insight, that peculiar consciousness" of the poet is derived from living Nature. It is what Emerson calls "The divine aura which breathes through forms."[54] The divine aura expresses itself through Imagination, which is a very high sort of seeing. The poet, says Gibran, is

> Alone,
> He is clothed in simplicity
> And nourished by tenderness;
> He sits in Nature's lap learning to create,

[53] Young, p. 169.
[54] Ralph Waldo Emerson, "The Poet," American Heritage, Vol. I (Boston: D. C. Heath and Company, 1955), p. 646.

And is awake in the stillness of the night
In wait of the spirit's descent.[55]

CIVILIZATION

Gibran devoted his life, as many men in history have done, to giving expression to words which awaken in mankind the significance of their deeds; by making them conscious of the existence of truth amid the falsity in their actual behavior, he makes his contribution to the advancement of civilization. Gibran's first utterances were vehement condemnations, which changed later to painful lamentations, and finally to a lucid understanding that society can be changed only when individuals in society become enlightened singly and then collectively.

In a very early work, Gibran wrote of slavery. He personified slavery, making an idol of it. He said, in effect, that people, rather than participating freely and fearlessly in life, are actually slaves of life, fettered to a crystallized image of it. Each person, being a slave in thought to another person, makes slavery in life his means and end rather than making freedom in life his means and his end.

I saw slavery over all, in a glorious and majestic procession of ignorance. I saw the people sacrificing the youths and maidens at the feet of the idol, calling her the God; pouring wine and perfume upon her feet, and calling her the queen; burning incense before her image, and calling her the Prophet; kneeling and worshipping before her, and calling her the Law; fighting and dying for her, and calling her Patriotism; submitting to her will, and calling her the Shadow of God on

[55] Kahlil Gibran, *A Tear and A Smile*, H. M. Nahmad, trans. (New York: Alfred A. Knopf, 1950), p. 135.

earth; destroying and demolishing homes and institutions for her sake, and calling her Fraternity; struggling and stealing and working for her, and calling her Fortune and Happiness; killing for her, and calling her Equality.

She possesses various names, but one reality. She has many appearances, but is made of one element. In truth she is an everlasting ailment bequeathed by each generation unto its successor.[56]

And what of Liberty? Weary, tired of beholding the processions of people who are deaf and dumb as stone, the poet walks alone in the night brooding over the ghosts of the past. Suddenly, he sees before him a dying, ghastly figure falling on her knees. He approaches near her and asks her name.

"My name is Liberty," replied this ghastly shadow of a corpse.

And I inquired, "Where are your children?"

And Liberty, tearful and weak, gasped, "One died crucified, another died mad, and the third is not yet born."

She limped away and spoke further, but the mist in my eyes and cries of my heart prevented sight or hearing.[57]

Lament over the glorification of slavery and the neglect of freedom is expressed again in a parabolic poem ironically called "The Perfect World."[58] The poet cries out to the God of lost souls, he who is lost among man's gods, to hear him. To this gentle Destiny that watches over the

[56] Kahlil Gibran, Secrets of the Heart, Anthony R. Ferris, trans. (New York: Philosophical Library, 1947), p. 31.
[57] Ibid., p. 34.
[58] The Madman, p. 69.

mad, wandering spirit of man he addresses his supplication and his lament. The poet begins by describing "the perfect world" wherein he lives. He is confused and out of harmony with the perfect race in the perfect world. The people have rigid laws of apparent completeness and order. All their thoughts are categorized and arranged, enrolled and registered. Virtues are measured and sins are weighed and even those things which are neither virtue nor sin are given names and catalogued. Even peoples' actions during the day and night are encompassed by rules of blameless accuracy. What to eat, what to drink, the proper clothes to wear, the time to work, to play, to sing, to dance—all these things are prescribed according to law. Even thoughts and feelings are controlled according to law. Pretentious behavior is made into doctrine in order

> to rob a neighbor with a smile, to bestow gifts with a graceful wave of the hand, to praise prudently, to blame cautiously, to destroy a soul with a word, to burn a body with a breath, and then to wash the hands when the day's work is done.[59]

Love is regulated in accord with preconceived rules, manners are prescribed by custom, the worship of the gods is properly conducted, and the devil is skillfully outwitted. Then all these actions may be forgotten and erased from memory. One has to think and to contemplate with a motive, a specific result, to be happy sweetly, to suffer graciously, and then to discard immediately all these reactions as if they are of no consequence and begin again tomorrow in the same manner.

> All these things, O God, are conceived with forethought, born with determination, nursed with exact-

[59] *Ibid.*, p. 70.

ness, governed by rules, directed by reason, and then
slain and buried after a prescribed method. And even
their silent graves that lie within the human soul are
marked and numbered.

It is a perfect world, a world of consummate excel-
lence, a world of supreme wonders, the ripest fruit in
God's garden, the master-thought of the universe.

But why should I be here, O God, I a green seed of
unfulfilled passion, a mad tempest that seeketh neither
east nor west, a bewildered fragment from a burnt
planet?

Why am I here, O God of lost souls, thou who art
lost among the gods?[60]

Here we find the perennial question which has been
asked by men in all ages—the "why?" of existence. Can
man ever know the answer to his "why"? Perhaps not, perhaps all man can do is to improve himself and in that attempt initiate the improvement of mankind. Gibran's works
are testimony of his contributions to the betterment of
relations among men. It is for man individually to accept
Gibran's concepts by making use of them or to reject them
by ignoring them; the choice is man's alone. The poet can
only point out, because of his perceptive ethereal awareness,
the offending practices. It is these practices that Gibran
describes and laments in "The Perfect World."

It is apparent that Gibran refers to America as the
perfect world of man-made order where God is suppressed
and hidden among man's gods. All spontaneity is lost and
is replaced by determinism. There is no feeling of responsibility for one's actions, for one "washes the hands when
day is done." Gibran's message is primarily one of awareness, and the secondary lesson is a corollary of the first. As

[60] *Ibid.*, p. 71.

the poet becomes aware of existing conditions, he realizes that he disapproves of them. In his disapproval and the weakness of his single condition, he rebels, and in his rebellion he cries out for meaning. There seems to be one ray of light in his dilemma; he recognizes, amid all his protestations, that America is "a world of supreme wonders, the ripest fruit in God's garden, the master-thought of the universe." Gibran was quoted as comparing America to a bud on the rosebush of life—a bud that is pressing its sheath, ready to open. However, it is "still hard, still green, and not yet fragrant, but vigorous and full of life."[61]

As a contrast to the knowledge of conditions in the perfect world, Gibran wrote the parable "God's Fool."[62] One day a man who was a dreamer came from the desert to the city of Sharia. He had only the clothes he wore and a staff. As he walked about the streets of the city, he gazed in wonder at the great temples and towers and palaces. He was amazed at their great beauty. Sometimes he would stop to speak to the people, asking them about their city. They could not answer him, for they did not understand his language, nor he theirs.

At noon he stopped before a great inn. It was beautifully built of yellow marble, and people were entering and leaving unhampered. He thought to himself that this must be a great shrine. He entered and was surprised to see numbers of men and women seated about many tables. It was a magnificent room, and the people in it were eating and drinking and listening to the musicians. This was no shrine, thought the dreamer, for he could not see anyone worshiping. Instead it must be a feast given by the prince for his people. They must be celebrating a great event. He stood thinking all these thoughts when a man, who he thought must be a slave of the prince, approached him and

[61] *Supra*, p. 38.
[62] The Forerunner, p. 9.

offered him a chair. He was served a delicious meal, complete with meat and wine and tasty sweets. He ate heartily, and then he rose to leave. He was stopped at the door by a man magnificently dressed. This, thought he, is the prince himself bidding me farewell. The dreamer bowed to him and thanked him.

"Sir, you have not paid for your dinner,"[63] said the man. Of course, the dreamer did not understand the language, so he bowed again and thanked the man heartily. The man looked at the dreamer more closely. He saw that he was a stranger, poorly dressed, and that indeed he had no money to pay for his meal. He clapped his hands and immediately four watchmen appeared. They listened to the directions of the large man. Then they approached the dreamer and put him between them and marched him out. The dreamer looked at their splendid uniforms and thought to himself that these were men of distinction and he became proud to walk with them.

They walked until they came to the House of Judgment. They went in and soon the dreamer saw before him a venerable man sitting on a throne. The man had a long flowing beard, and his robe was majestic. Surely, he thought, this is the king, and he was delighted to be brought before him. He stood watching as he listened to the watchmen talking to the king. He did not understand that they were relating to the judge the charges against him, nor that the judge appointed two advocates, one to present the charge against him and one to defend him. He remained quietly but joyfully listening to the arguments of the advocates, and the dreamer thought he was listening to addresses of welcome. He was overcome with gratitude for the king and the prince for the wonderful things that were happening to him.

[63] *Ibid.*, p. 10.

*Then sentence was passed upon the dreamer, that
upon a tablet hung about his neck his crime should be
written, and that he should ride through the city on a
naked horse, with a trumpeter and a drummer before
him. And the sentence was carried out forthwith.*[64]

The dreamer gladly performed whatever was required
of him. As he rode through the city on the naked horse
with the noise of the trumpeter and the drummer before
him, the people came running out at the sounds which
disturbed their peace. Everyone was laughing at him, and
the children ran after him in groups from street to street.
The dreamer was so happy tears filled his eyes, for he
thought that the tablet about his neck was a sign of the
king's blessing and the procession was certainly in his honor.

As he was riding down the streets of the city, he saw
among the crowd a man from the desert just like himself,
and in his joy, he called to him:

*"Friend! Friend! Where are we? What city of the
heart's desire is this? What race of lavish hosts?—Who
feast the chance guest in their palaces, whose princes
companion him, whose king hangs a token upon his
breast and opens to him the hospitality of a city
descended from heaven."*

*And he who was also of the desert replied not. He
only smiled and slightly shook his head. And the procession passed on.*

*And the dreamer's face was uplifted and his eyes
were overflowing with light.*[65]

The title of this parable, "God's Fool," gives a clue to
the spiritual lesson. The first conclusion one likely reaches
takes into account the obvious naivete or ignorance of the

[64] *Ibid.*, p. 12.
[65] *Ibid.*, pp. 13-14.

dreamer. One thing is noticeable: the treatment he was subjected to, although ridiculous, was not physically painful. He was left free to think as he wished. Insofar as he was not aware of the psychological implications of the people's actions, he was permitted to think they were good, and that fact delighted him. Indeed he is life's fool. Perhaps, that is why he is a dreamer and why he is also God's fool. The lesson lies in the desirability of dreaming about life; no matter how foolish one's dreams may seem, he finds joy and comfort in them.

The actions of the people seem realistic. Perhaps, the inability to pay for one meal would not entail such punishment, but that fact is incidental to the narrative. One may also regard the actions of the restaurant owner, policemen, judge, and people as absurd, but so are the actions of much of society today. Society's ritualistic laws must be performed and so they were.

The last narrative relating to organic civilization concerns "Peace and War."[66] The characters are dogs and the kingdom is dogdom. Since the lesson this parable expresses applies directly to the present discussion, it is recounted here.

One day three dogs were sitting together enjoying the sun and talking. One dog said dreamily that it was wonderful to be living at that time in the world of dogdom. He pointed to the ease of travel on earth, on sea, and in the air. He spoke of the inventions that made a dog's life increasingly comfortable, and brought pleasure to his eyes and ears and nose.

Whereupon the second dog spoke, bringing attention to all dogs' increased awareness of the arts. Dogs could bark more rhythmically at the moon than their forefathers had done, and when dogs looked at themselves in the water, they could see themselves more clearly.

[66] The Wanderer, p. 30.

*Then the third dog spoke and said, "But what inter-
ests me most and beguiles my mind is the tranquil
understanding existing between dogdoms."*

*At that very moment they looked, and lo, the dog
catcher was approaching.*

*The three dogs sprang up and scampered down the
street; and as they ran the third dog said, "For God's
sake, run for your lives. Civilization is after us."*[67]

"Yea, ye are laughable unto me, ye present-day men!
And especially when ye marvel at yourselves!,"[68] said Nietzsche. Gibran also laughs at present-day men and their
so-called achievements. Civilization has given man practically all the material comforts of life, but the things most
desired—peace and good-will among men—have not been
achieved. Those in authority may still demand the forfeit
of a man's life. The existence of understanding between
nations is illusionary. Man has progressed materially, but
spiritually he has not. He has transferred his allegiance from
one purpose to many purposes, from the quest of truth to
idols of destruction. He has veiled truth. Man has sought
perfection in the material comforts of life. He has improved
his mode of travel from the laborious and slow pace of
walking to greater and faster modes of travel by land, sea,
and air.

Man has found increased value in the arts. Now he
speaks in modulated tones and knows of what he speaks.
And he knows more about himself, for his physical characteristics are clearer to him now. Most of all, there is apparent peace and understanding among nations. However, all
of these arguments for man's progress do not alter the

[67] *Ibid.*, pp. 30-31.
[68] Friedrich Nietzsche, "Thus Spake Zarathustra," Thomas Common,
trans., *The Philosophy of Nietzsche* (New York: The Modern Library,
1954), p. 131.

irreducible fact of man's brutality and propensity toward destruction. In short, the lesson of the parable is the need for awareness of both man's intelligence and man's ignorance. Since man has both, perhaps his intelligence may recognize his ignorance. This fact is always a probability. Erich Fromm says, "The dynamism of man's nature is an important factor that tends to seek for more satisfying solutions if there is a possibility of attaining them."[69] Gibran also recognizes the ability of man to discover new solutions, and there is the possibility that now an increasing number of men are also recognizing this fact. Gibran said, "There is a new whisper of life upon the firmament."[70]

THE AWAKENING

Gibran repeats the maxim that man's spiritual awakening is unveiled, insofar as it can be unveiled or known, in the perceptive understanding of life experiences. Man takes the familiar and actual moment of existence, that is, of being consciously alive and acting each moment of each day, as a means only to some distant end. Mere living in the present has no immediate importance. Gibran emphasizes emphatically the spiritual significance, the vision or the dream as he calls it, in everyday living and everyday acting. Ibn Khaldûn, an Arab scholar and historian of the fourteenth century, offers this explanation:

The arguments concerning the existentia beyond sensual perception—the spiritualia—constitute what the (philosophers) call "the divine science" or science of metaphysics. The essences of (the spiritualia) are

[69] Erich Fromm, Escape from Freedom (New York: Holt, Rinehart and Winston, 1961), p. 238.
[70] Young, p. 132.

completely unknown. One cannot get at them, nor can they be proven by logical arguments, because an abstraction of intelligibilia from the individual existentia of the outside world is possible only in the case of things we can perceive by the senses, from which the universals are thus derived. We cannot perceive the spiritual essences and abstract further quiddities from them, because the senses constitute a veil between us and them. We have, thus, no (logical) arguments for them, and we have no way whatever of affirming their existence. There are only available to us (in this connection) the situations in which perceptions of the human soul take place, and especially the dream visions which are within the intuitive experience of all.[71]

Therefore, as long as man continues to direct his life in accord with sensual perceptions, he creates a veil between the spiritual essence and himself. There is no argument that one can give to verify this statement. However, if man becomes aware that he is using only the senses for the acquisition of knowledge and pleasure, he may, at the same time, become aware of his thinking—in Ibn Khaldûn's words "dream visions," in Gibran's words "waking dreams."[72] Thus man in awareness discovers a situation "in which perceptions of the human soul take place." With this awakening of the human soul, situations in which misunderstandings and cruelties exist are resolved. Much of man's cruelty is self-inflicted, in many instances, through his misinterpretations of the written word, especially the words of Scripture.

In Gibran's parable "The Blessed City,"[73] he describes

[71] Ibn Khaldûn, *The Muqaddiman, An Introduction to History*, Franz Rosenthal, trans. in 3 Vols., Vol. III (New York: Bollingen Foundation, Inc., 1958), p. 252.
[72] *The Garden of the Prophet*, p. 16.
[73] *The Madman*, p. 42.

a city where everyone lived according to the Scriptures. A man, in his youth, had heard about a Blessed City, and in later life wanted desperately to see it. It was a distant city; therefore provisions for a long journey were acquired. He traveled for forty days; on the forty-first day he entered the city.

"And lo! the whole company of the inhabitants had each but a single eye and but one hand."[74] He was amazed at what he saw. They, too, were astonished to see that he had two hands and two eyes. He approached them and inquired if this was indeed the Blessed City where each man lived according to the Scriptures. And they answered that it was. Then he asked them what had befallen them, and where were their right eyes and their right hands. Touched by his questions, they said that they would show him. They took him to the temple which was in the center of the city.

And in the temple I saw a heap of hands and eyes. All withered. Then I said, "Alas, what conqueror had committed this cruelty upon you?"

And there went a murmur amongst them. And one of their elders stood forth and said, "This doing is of ourselves. God had made us conquerors over the evil that was in us."

And he led me to a high altar, and all the people followed. And he showed me above the altar an inscription graven, and I read:

If thy right eye offend thee, pluck it out and cast it from thee; for it is profitable for thee that one of thy members should perish, and not that thy whole body should be cast into hell. And if thy right hand offend thee, cut it off and cast it from thee; for it is profitable for thee that one of thy members should perish, and

[74] *Ibid.*

not that thy whole body should be cast into hell."
Then I understood. And I turned about to all the
people and cried, "Hath no man or woman among you
two eyes or two hands?"
And they answered me saying, "No, not one. There
is none whole save such as are yet too young to read
the Scripture and to understand its commandment."
And when we had come out of the temple, I
straightway left that Blessed City; for I was not too
young, and I could read the Scripture.[75]

The literal interpretation of the Scriptures has caused
man to commit untold cruelties on man with holy sanc-
tions. The declaration "An eye for an eye, tooth for a tooth,
hand for hand, foot for foot, burning for burning, wound
for wound, stripe for stripe"[76] has caused much suffering
and agony since its first utterance. Even today, men mis-
understand the symbolic meanings of Scriptural words. The
meaning of "If thy right eye offend thee, pluck it out and
cast it from thee," and "If thy right hand offend thee, cut
it off and cast it from thee" obviously is not to be applied
literally. It would be against the teaching of love that the
Scriptures are based upon.

The verb "offend" means to cause dislike or anger, or
to oppose or obstruct in duty. If we assume that "offend"
means to oppose or obstruct one's actions, and if we assume
further that rather than to the organ called "eye" or to the
organ called "hand," the words apply to the action of the
eye, that is, what the eye sees, and the action of the hand,
what it does, then we can say that these admonitions can
mean: If we see or become aware of something in everyday
life which obstructs us in our actions and our knowledge of

[75] *Ibid.,* pp. 43-44.
[76] Exodus 21:24, 25.

actions, then we should leave it or cast it away from us for it is better to throw off one thing, no matter if it is as dear to us as an eye or a hand might be, rather than to keep it and have it destroy or corrupt our whole body. Likewise, if we perform an action of which we are ashamed, it is better to "cut it off" or forget it completely rather than let the memory of it disrupt and corrupt our whole body, our entire life. Actions once performed are dead actions, and obstacles which cannot be surmounted should be left alone. From this concept is derived the spiritual lesson of Gibran's parable.

The name of the city is quite ironic, but the people thought that they were being blessed in carrying out the instructions of the Scriptures to the letter. They were performing these cruelties on themselves because they considered that they themselves were evil. They thought God had made them conquerors over evil, and the manner of conquerors is to punish. Again they were giving a literal interpretation of the Scripture, which cautions against such misunderstandings.

> Who [God] also hath made us able ministers of the new testament; not of the letter, but of the spirit; for the letter killeth, but the spirit giveth life.[77]

The discovery of the power of the spirit to change one's view of life is essayed in the parable "The Last Watch."[78] It is a parable of lamentation and awakening. In the small hours of the night before the faint light of dawn appeared, the Forerunner, "he who calls himself echo to a voice yet unheard,"[79] left his bed and ascended to the roof of his home. He stood and gazed down upon the sleep-

[77] 2 Corinthians 3:6.
[78] *The Forerunner*, p. 57.
[79] *Ibid.*

ing city. Finally he raised his head, "and even as if the
sleepless spirits of all those asleep had gathered around
him,"[80] he began to speak. He addressed them as his friends
and neighbors and those who merely walked by his gate.
He told them that he would rather speak to them while
they were sleeping or dreaming, for then he can "walk
naked," that is, feel free and unrestrained. In their waking
hours, they were too busy to listen, and there was too much
noise for them to hear.

The Forerunner wanted desperately to speak to them
of his love for them and the suffering he had endured
because of it. "I love the one among you as though he were
all, and all as if you were one."[81] He told them he had loved
them in his youth and also in his maturity. Then he began
to single out each one separately and declared his love for
each. He loved "the giant and the pigmy, the leper and
the anointed,"[82] in other words, the great and the small,
the cursed and the blessed. He loved him who was blind in
ignorance and him who was happy in the light. He loved
the strong even though the Forerunner had felt their iron
hoofs on his flesh; he loved the weak even though they had
exhausted his faith ·and wasted his patience. He loved the
rich, although their honey was bitter to his mouth, and he
loved the poor, although the poor knew the Forerunner's
empty-handed shame.

He loved the poet even though his song was borrowed
and his composition was blind, for his love for the poet was
self-indulgence. He loved the scholar even though the
scholar was one who gathered "rotted shrouds in potters'
fields."[83] He loved the priest who sat in the dead silences

[80] *Ibid.*
[81] *Ibid.*, p. 58.
[82] *Ibid.*
[83] *Ibid.*

of yesterday as the priest questioned the promise of the Forerunner's future. He loved the worshippers, though they worshipped gods who were the images of their own desires.

He loved the "thirsting woman whose cup is ever full,"[84] for he understood her; and the woman of restless nights, he loved her in pity.

> You the talkative have I loved, saying, "Life hath much to say"; and you the dumb have I loved, whispering to myself, "Says he not in silence that which I fain would hear in words?"
>
> And you the judge and critic, I have loved also; yet when you have seen me crucified, you said, "He bleeds rhythmically, and the pattern his blood makes upon his white skin is beautiful to behold."[85]

He loved the young and the old, the weak and the strong, but, alas, the over-abundance of his love had turned them from him.

> You would drink love from a cup, but not from a surging river. You would hear love's faint murmur, but when love shouts you would muffle your ears.
>
> And because I have loved you all you have said, "Too soft and yielding is his heart, and too undiscerning is his path. It is the love of a needy one, who picks crumbs even as he sits at kingly feasts. And it is the love of a weakling, for the strong loves only the strong."[86]

The Forerunner continued in his lament, saying that the people said his great love for them was but the love of a blind man who could not differentiate between the beauty

[84] *Ibid.*, p. 59.
[85] *Ibid.*
[86] *Ibid.*, p. 60.

of one man and the ugliness of another. They said that his love could not distinguish between vinegar and wine. They said that his love was impertinent and overweening, for what stranger could be all things to them as their mother and father, their sister and brother. All these things they said of him, and they often pointed their fingers at him and mocked him.

There goes the ageless one, the man without seasons, who at the noon hour plays games with our children and at eventide sits with our elders and assumes wisdom and understanding.[87]

In spite of all their misconceptions, the Forerunner had previously said to himself that he would love them ever more. But he had decided to hide his love with seeming hate, and to disguise his tenderness as bitterness. He had put on an iron mask, and only then when he was controlled and fully protected was he able to seek them. Arrayed in armor, he had heaped assaults on them. He had struck them in their wounds, and like a tempest he had thundered in their ears. From the housetops he had proclaimed them "hypocrites, Pharisees, tricksters, false and empty earth-bubbles."[88] The shortsighted he had cursed for being blind bats, and the earthy ones he had compared to soulless moles. The eloquent of speech he had described as fork-tongued, the silent as stone-lipped, and the simple and naive as the dead and those that are never weary of death. Those who sought world knowledge he had condemned as violators of the holy spirit, and those who sought the spirit were branded as hunters of shadows who cast their nets into shallow waters and caught only their own images.

Thus with my lips have I denounced you, while my

[87] *Ibid.*, p. 61.
[88] *Ibid.*

heart, bleeding within me, called you tender names.
It was love lashed by its own self that spoke. It was
pride half slain that fluttered in the dust. It was my
hunger for your love that raged from the housetop,
while my own love, kneeling in silence, prayed your
forgiveness.

But behold a miracle!

It was my disguise that opened your eyes, and my
seeming to hate that woke your hearts.

And now you love me.

You love the swords that strike you and the arrows
that crave your breast. For it comforts you to be
wounded and only when you drink of your own blood
can you be intoxicated.[89]

After saying these things, the Forerunner compared
the people to moths that seek the flame which destroys
them. They, too, gathered about him with their faces uplifted and their eyes enchanted while he tore the very fabric
of their days. In their delight they said that he saw with the
light of God, that he was like the prophets of old, that he
ripped the veils that covered their souls, and he unlocked
the door of their hearts; "and like the eagle that knows the
way of foxes he knows their ways."[90]

Yes, he had answered, he knew their ways but only as
the eagle knew the ways of his fledglings. He wanted to tell
them his secret: it was because he had need of their near-
ness that he feigned remoteness, and it was because he
feared the subsiding of their love for him that he guarded
the overflow of his own love.

After saying these things the Forerunner covered
his face with his hands and wept bitterly. For he knew

[89] Ibid., pp. 62-63.
[90] Ibid.

*in his heart that love humiliated in its nakedness is
greater than love that seeks triumph in disguise; and
he was ashamed.*

*But suddenly he raised his head, and like one wak-
ing from sleep he outstretched his arms and said,
"Night is over, and we children of night must die
when dawn comes leaping upon the hills; and out of
our ashes a mightier love shall rise. And it shall laugh
in the sun, and it shall be deathless."*[91]

The Forerunner's agony has passed, the catharsis is
completed, and he is purified.

*He who would seek Truth and proclaim it to man-
kind is bound to suffer. My sorrows have taught me
to understand the sorrows of my fellow men . . .
persecution . . . [has not] dimmed the vision within
me.*[92]

Thus Gibran declares the message of "The Forerunner." The night of despair it over: it is dead, and from
its ashes a mightier love is born. The poet has found "a
love that revealed the hidden things of the spirit to the
spirit, and by its actions separated the mind from the
regions of measurement and weight."[93] There is no need
for judging and condemning; the Forerunner has awakened
to a Greater Self, a new understanding. He is content. He
is free. Now he can laugh in the light of the sun.

Those who would be as hermits and protect themselves from relationships with others are not prepared to
speak on the meaning of life. Gibran exemplifies this prin-

[91] *Ibid.,* pp. 63-64.
[92] Kahlil Gibran, *The Voice of the Master,* trans. Anthony R. Ferris
(New York: The Citadel Press, 1958), p. 25.
[93] Kahlil Gibran, *Nymphs of the Valley,* trans. H. M. Nahmad (New
York: Alfred A. Knopf, 1948), p. 38.

ciple in the parable "The Hermit and the Beasts."[94] "Once
there lived among the green hills a hermit. He was pure
of spirit and white of heart."[95] The animals and the birds
delighted in him. They came to him in pairs, and he spoke
to them. The animals listened to him with open hearts,
and they stayed near him until he sent them away, "en-
trusting them to the wind and the woods with his blessing."[96]

One evening as he was speaking to them of love, a
leopard raised her head and asked him,

> "You speak to us of loving. Tell us, Sir, where is
> your mate?"
> And the hermit said, "I have no mate."
> Then a great cry of surprise rose from the company
> of beasts and fowls, and they began to say among
> themselves, "How can he tell us of loving and mating
> when he himself knows naught thereof?" And quietly
> and in disdain they left him alone.
> That night the hermit lay upon his mat with his
> face earthward, and he wept bitterly and he beat his
> hands upon his breast.[97]

The hermit is described as being a pure and an up-
right man. He lived in the security of his green hills, en-
trusting the animals to the wind and the woods, the
vicissitudes of fortune. As for himself, he refrained from
immersing in the destructive element. Isolated, mateless,
he had dared to speak of love and the experience of loving
to animals. The animals represent the uncontrolled natural
tendencies of man as opposed to the suppressed natural
tendencies of the ascetic man. Since man is both animal

[94] *The Wanderer*, p. 16.
[95] *Ibid.*
[96] *Ibid.*
[97] *Ibid.*, pp. 16-17.

and spiritual, one part of his nature suffers if it is not
coordinated with the other part. To know his animal
nature, man must sound its depths in life experiences,
cognizant of the possible destructiveness of his quest. Concerning sex, Gibran said, "I do not know what in this
world is not sex, do you? Only the little stones in the
riverbed, perhaps, and the blown sands upon the shores
of the great seas."[98] Intelligent man is the path between his
lower or animal nature and his higher or spiritual nature.
Therefore, it is in the participation in all forms of experiences without fear that man learns the essence of earthly
life. In many and various words Jesus told his disciples,
"The kingdom of the Father is spread upon the earth and
men do not see it."[99]

It is upon the good earth that man is born, lives, and
dies. Whatever experiences man has are life experiences.
That is all that man can know. However, for some unex-
plainable reason, man partakes of an unobservable Force
in the universe, a Force that moves and has its being in
man whether he is aware of it or not. In the movements
and manifestations of this Force, man affects his own life
and the lives of others. Man is alone and man is not alone.
Man is alone in that he participates in this Force directly
without an intermediary. He is not alone in that he exists
on earth with others—others whom he needs. Man's silent
needs give meaning to his life, a meaning embodied in the
body and spirit of man. To recognize that man is both
body and spirit, to harmonize these two aspects of his
character, and to act in accord with this harmony is the
awakening of man's wisdom. Meanwhile, absurd cruelties

[98] *Supra*, p. 36.
[99] A. Guillaumont and others, translators, *The Gospel According to
Thomas* (New York: Harper and Brothers, 1959), Sec. 99: 1s. 16-18, p.
57. These "sayings of Jesus" were contained in the discovery of a Coptic
library in Upper Egypt, 1945.

perpetrated by man on man continue. The body, the crucible of the Most High, is corrupted by acts more brutal than the acts of beasts and with less reason. To kill, to wound, to crucify has been the mode of existence. Why then does man prevail? There is no answer. There is only a possible awareness of the Dignity, the Most High, in man, and that endures. It is Life reflected in life. It is what Gibran observes and describes in his parables. It is what Gibran means when he says:

> You are spirits though you move in bodies; and, like oil that burns in the dark, you are flames though held in lamps.
>
> If you were naught save bodies, then my standing before you and speaking unto you would be but emptiness, even as the dead calling unto the dead. But this is not so. All that is deathless in you is free unto the day and the night and cannot be housed nor fettered, for this is the will of the Most High. You are His breath even as the wind that shall be neither caught nor caged. And I also am the breath of His breath.[100]

Gibran's final message proclaims the spiritual relatedness of man in society. This final stage of understanding is reached after much inner conflict. Gibran's line of development has been followed from his first angry and denunciatory writings in The Madman, to the transitional phase of description and lament in The Forerunner, and finally to the mellow wisdom exemplified in The Wanderer. The parables serve not only as a means of communicating Gibran's inner thoughts and feelings, but also as a vehicle which enables the reader to perceive the successive stages of change in Gibran's social concepts. Gibran came to realize that for man to change society, condemnation of

[100] The Garden of the Prophet, pp. 25-26.

society is not enough. First man must understand himself in relation to society, then the right transformation can take place, first in himself, then in society. Relatedness, then, is a form of uniting man with himself and with his fellow man. It is accomplished through the observations of one's own thoughts and actions and the results of these actions on others. This is the last step in Gibran's development and the concluding spiritual message of his parables.

3

Parables in Gibran's Art

GIBRAN WAS BOTH poet and artist. His art like
his writings portrays his inner feelings concerning man in
interaction with man. Since sixteen books out of a possible
twenty are illustrated with his drawings, I deemed it necessary to attempt an interpretation of his drawings and to
correlate them with his writings, especially with his parables.

Gibran's art may be approached in the same manner
as his parables. The definition of the parable has been given
as a fictitious narrative or allegory of "events in human life
or of a process in nature, by which some great spiritual
truth is illustrated or enforced."[1] Gibran's drawings portray
movement. The movement is suggested by the intended
action of human bodies. The action, being an event or a
happening in human life, is therefore a life experience with
outward movement suggesting the inward or spiritual
movement. Rather than using words, the artist employs
lines and shadows to convey his impressions of life proc-

[1] *Supra*, p. 46.

esses. The purpose of Gibran's parabolic art is twofold: first, to express and to portray the struggles of his own inner life, and secondly, there is an earnest desire that others may be awakened to know and to express their own inner life. Perhaps in this awakened state of awareness, man can begin to resolve many of his conflicts and problems. "O my brother, every problem that has troubled you has troubled me,"[2] Gibran said.

Gibran, as artist, dispenses with decorative detail in his art. Moreover, the background is clear of all plant life and all material objects, indicating the indefiniteness of the place and time of action. His drawings are simple, honest, aimed directly at the revelation of the universal spiritual lesson embodied in the natural processes of life. Alice Raphael, in her discussion of Gibran's art, sets forth the province of the artist.

Life in its elemental functioning is but a transformation of the processes of birth, love, and death. The hunger of the appetites and the hunger of possession; the desire for adventure and the fear of the unknown; to love and be loved; out of these essential simplicities, man has erected the vast complexities of life and to these essential simplicities the artist must return who seeks new means of expression amidst the clutter of religions, arts and moralities.[3]

Gibran represents in his art as he does in his parables the essential simplicities which are a part of everyday living. Similar to the understanding of the written parable, one must possess the a priori knowledge to grasp the spiritual import the parable suggests. However, the meaning is not difficult to comprehend if one bears in mind the spiritual connectiveness of man. Gibran portrays again the existent

oneness of man in his personal relationship to Universal
Life. Life is represented as the All-Mother of the Universe,
the Creative Spirit. Gibran once said,

> "Everything in nature bespeaks the mother. The
> sun is the mother of earth and gives it its nourishment
> of heat; it never leaves the universe at night until it
> has put the earth to sleep to the song of the sea and
> the hymn of birds and brooks. And this earth is the
> mother of trees and flowers. It produces them. The
> trees and flowers become mothers of their great fruits
> and seeds. And the mother, the prototype of all exist-
> ence, is the eternal spirit, full of beauty and love.[4]

However, the recognition of beauty must begin with
man himself. In the following several pages, conversations
are recounted between Gibran and Mary Haskell and
Gibran and Mikhail Naimy for two reasons: first, because
very little critical material could be found on Gibran's
art, and secondly, it was felt that Gibran's personal views
on the purpose of art and the artist needed presentation to
illuminate and consequently to clarify Gibran's particular
style of art.

Gibran told Mary Haskell early in their friendship,
"Beauty is that harmony between joy and sorrow which
begins in our holy of holies and ends beyond the scope of
our imagination."[5] That is to say, the holy of holies, which
is the body, harmonizes the emotions of joy and sorrow so
that a beautiful experience is felt which elevates the imagination beyond the power of description. In addition,
Gibran says that beauty is a power which leads man's
heart to the throne of "Women which is the throne of
God."[6] Miss Haskell was taken aback and told him that

[4] *Kahlil Gibran: A Self Portrait*, p. 9.
[5] Naimy, p. 62.
[6] Ibid.

he exalted "woman far too high by making her throne and
God's one."[7] Gibran answered:

> Most religions speak of God in the masculine
> gender. To me He is as much a mother as He is a
> Father. He is both the father and the mother in one;
> and Woman is the God-Mother. The God-Father
> may be reached through the mind or the imagination.
> But the God-Mother can be reached through the heart
> only—through love. And Love is that holy wine which
> the gods distill from their hearts and pour into the
> hearts of men. Those only taste it pure and divine
> whose hearts have been cleansed of all the animal
> lusts. For clean hearts to be drunk with love is to be
> drunk with God. Those, on the other hand, who drink
> it mixed with the wines of earthly passions taste but
> the orgies of devils in Hell.[8]

It has been shown that Gibran suffered much because
of his love and his passions. It was precisely these earthly
passions in addition to his ill-health that Gibran grappled
with practically all his life. A few months before his death,
Gibran, ill and weary, discussed beauty and art and their
manifestations, this time with his close friend Naimy.
Naimy, shocked at seeing Gibran's pallor and fatigue,
cautioned him against continued work. Gibran immediately
rejected Naimy's advice, saying his life would be worthless
without writing and drawing and that Naimy should know
that. Gibran asked,

> "Must one choke the poetry and art in us in order
> to spare the breath in our nostrils?"

Naimy replied:

> "Art is the realizing of the harmony of being in our

[7] Ibid.
[8] Ibid., p. 62.

own spirits and of translating that harmony into aims,
thoughts, and deeds which leave no room for friction
in our souls between good and evil . . .

So long as we pass through states which so crush
the heart and muddle the mind as to cloud our sight,
and turn the honey in our mouths into gall, and dis-
joint our joints—what good is the good of a beautiful
picture we draw, or of a ringing poem we write? Can
we draw Beauty unless it draws us first? Can we utter
Truth before Truth has uttered to us? If we but live
a beautiful life, we should do nothing but the beautiful; and then we should have no need of drawing
Beauty. Did we obey the Truth in our thoughts, we
should be able to utter nothing but the Truth; and
then we should have no need to preach the Truth."

And Gibran answered:

"Is it not true, Mischa, that every time we draw
Beauty we approach a step nearer to Beauty? And
every time we write the Truth we become one with
it? Or do you propose to muzzle poets and artists?
Is not self-expression a deeply seated need in the
human soul?"[9]

Naimy replied that Truth is free only to radiate its
secrets. As soon as we try, Naimy continued, to give expression to those secrets whether in words or in painting, we
"disfigure them by either adding to them or subtracting
from them; they are never the same when expressed as
when unexpressed."[10]

Naimy pointed out that the beauty which is sup-
posedly extricated from ugliness is not beauty, neither can
the ugliness which coexists with beauty be ugliness. Further

[9] *Ibid.*, p. 233.
[10] *Ibid.*

Naimy said that, if man thinks he can sift the beautiful from the ugly, it is as if he says to the Creator of Life,

" 'You ill govern Your creation. You have confounded the true of it and the false, the beautiful and the ugly. Descend from Your throne and I shall show you how to winnow all things and gather the beautiful and the true unto the beautiful and the true, and the ugly and the false unto the ugly and the false!' Is not God beyond our notions of beauty and ugliness, and above our right and wrong?"

Gibran answered:

"He is, Mischa, He is. Perhaps we are nearer to Him each time we try to divide Him and find Him indivisible. Yet do I say that art, through drawing a line between the beautiful and the ugly, is the nearest way to God. Pure meditation which you seem to stress is another way. But it leads to silence and to self-confinement. You are right—silence is truer and more expressive than speech; and the hour shall come when we shall be silent. But why muzzle our tongues before that hour has struck? There is your friend Lao Tzu;[11] he became silent, but when? After he gave to the world the gist of his faith in words. Yea, we shall be silent some day, Mischa. But now let us speak."[12]

And speak Gibran did as truthfully and as sincerely as it was in his power to do in his words and in his drawings. Sometimes his artistic integrity gave him much trouble, especially when he was drawing women. They did not want to be portrayed as the artist's eyes saw them, but

[11] Lao Tzu was born in 600 B.C. He was a Chinese philosopher, from whom Confucious sought advice, and founder of the naturalistic, quietistic philosophy called Taoism, or Tao meaning the "way." "Lao Tzu." Encyclopedia Britannica, Vol. 13, p. 712.
[12] Naimy, p. 224.

as beautiful damsels who perhaps rivaled even the Venus de Milo. Gibran said,

> "*I should be a traitor to my art if I were to borrow my sitter's eyes. The face is a marvelous mirror that reflects most faithfully the innermost of the soul; the artist's business is to see that and portray it; otherwise he is not fit to be called an artist.*"[13]

Auguste Rodin, famous sculptor and Gibran's instructor while in Paris, said, "The artist . . . sees; that is to say, that his eye grafted on his heart, reads deeply into the bosom of Nature . . . The artist has only to trust his eyes."[14] Gibran was fascinated by Rodin's sculpture. Looking at Rodin's "The Hand of God," Gibran was compelled to ask,

> *Is it really God that created Man, or is it the opposite? Imagination is the only creator, its nearest and clearest manifestation is Art; yes, art is life, life is art; all else is trite and empty in comparison.*[15]

To Gibran "A work of art is a mist carved into an image."[16] In other words, a nebulous thought indistinct without form molded into a manifest image. One must remember that the image includes form which can be evident in the actual actions that exist in one's everyday behavior. It is a life image, for Gibran said, "Art is a step from nature toward the infinite."[17] It appears that all great artists have the same conception concerning art whether the image is conveyed in word or line. Robert Browning

[13] *Ibid.*, p. 182.
[14] Auguste Rodin, *On Art and Artists* (New York: Philosophical Library, 1957), p. 49. This book was translated from the French of Paul Gsell by Mrs. Romilly Feddin.
[15] Naimy, p. 87.
[16] Quoted by Young, p. 75.
[17] *Ibid.*

said, "All poetry being putting the infinite within the finite"[18] must of necessity be somewhat indefinite because of its inherent universality; and, "in asking for more ultimates, you must accept less mediates."[19] Therefore an artist must be evaluated not by self-expression alone, but by his ability to portray the timelessness of the universals which man aspires to know and which he symbolizes in his art. Alice Raphael says,

> The true symbolist is concerned with the life of the inner world. To his eyes the changing cultures are merely transformations upon which he focuses his attention. Whereas, to the ideationist—the objective artist—each epoch, each strata in the history of man is a separate and distant reality and he occupies himself depicting the surfaces and planes of the outer expression of life. He is in constant relation to the present; he has no personal affiliation with the vast spiritual life of the past and possesses no embryonic conception of the future.

> "But to the true symbolist life is a perpetual recreation and he moves in a world freed from traditions and confines. He need not attempt to escape from the limitations of the present by seeking the mannerisms of an enigmatical past. He is in direct contact with the past and hence the future is an ever fluid and ever luminous atmosphere; he is at one with fundamentals."[20]

Miss Raphael refers to the Primitives and the symbolism in their art. "They cared so deeply for the *spirit of the idea* that the manner of its presentation caused

---

[18] J. M. Cohen, *Robert Browning*, (New York: Longman's, Green and Co., 1952) p. 172.
[19] *Ibid.*
[20] "Introduction," *Twenty Drawings*, p. 8.

them little concern."[21] The Primitives covered the walls of Assisi with the story of Jesus, for they wished others to know of it and to profit by it.

To them, Jesus was a reality, not a story about which to make a painting, and consequently it was a matter of indifference to Ghirlandio whether the women attending the Virgin wore the dresses of his own age or those of antiquity. They were the women attending the Virgin and that which has given the Santa Maris Novella its lustre, is the power of a feeling, visioned, experienced, grasped—and then put forth again.[22]

Miss Raphael states further that in separating the symbolist from the ideationist, the art of the East is divided from the art of the West. To the man of the East all things bespeak a divinity, even a lotus flower. To the Western man the lotus is a flower which develops into an acanthus design, a decoration, and becomes again only a flower. The elements of the universe, the earth, the sun, the sea, all things above, and all things below are to the Western mind only materials for study to be touched, represented, understood, and grasped. To the Eastern man, these things are and they will be eternally, and behind these realities which one can see and know, "lie other and again other forces and experiences, other suns, other seas melting mysteriously into one another as the leaves of the lotus."[23]

It is at this dividing line of East and West, of the symbolist and the ideationist, that the work of Kahlil Gibran presents itself as an arresting type in our conception of painting. He has accepted both the traditions of form and the inner meaning of the idea, and

[21] *Ibid.,* the italics are mine.
[22] *Ibid.*
[23] *Ibid.,* p. 9.

*he exhibits both a new type of work and another
method of approach to fundamental truths.*[24]

Miss Raphael points out that there is no conflict in
Gibran's art as to "whether the idea shall prevail over the
emotion, or whether emotion shall sway the thought,"[25]
because both are so equally demonstrated that one is not
conscious one or the other is dominant. They coexist in
harmony and in that lies their beauty.

*An illuminating beauty informs his work; to him
the idea becomes beautiful if it is true; the emotion
becomes truth if it is real. And he keeps to a simplicity
of manner in the portrayal of an idea which is closely
akin to the spirit of the Primitives, albeit the art of the
centuries has gone into the moulding of his powers;
but in his statements he is simple, almost instinctively
simple.*[26]

Miss Raphael calls Gibran an intuitive artist, an artist
equipped with a divining rod which discovers golden values
and which "does not obfuscate his mind with intellectual
conceptions of what or how he should create."[27] Following
his ability for seeing truth, he then applies his conscious
powers to perfect his finding and to create his embryonic
expressions into paintings of beauty and value."[28]

Upon being asked why he chose that style of art,
Gibran said:

*Perhaps it chose me. Quite unconsciously, I found
myself walking that path; and each of us has his path.
When I began to draw and paint, I did not say to
myself, "Behold Kahlil Gibran. There are ahead of you
so many ways to art: The classic, the modern, the sym-*

[24] *Ibid.,* p. 10.
[25] *Ibid.*
[26] *Ibid.*
[27] *Ibid.,* p. 11.
[28] *Ibid.*

bolistic, the impressionistic, and others. Choose for
yourself one of them." I did nothing of the sort. I
simply found my pen and brush, quite of themselves,
recording symbols of my thoughts, emotions, and fan-
cies. Some think the business of art to be a mere imitation of nature. But Nature is far too great and too
subtle to be successfully imitated. No artist can ever re-
produce even the least of Nature's surpassing creations
and miracles. Besides, what profit is there in imitating
Nature when she is so open and so accessible to all
who see and hear? The business of art is rather to
understand Nature and to reveal her meanings to those
unable to understand. It is to convey the soul of a tree
rather than to produce a fruitful likeness of the tree.
It is to reveal the conscience of the sea, not to portray
so many foaming waves or so much blue water. The
mission of art is to bring out the unfamiliar from the
most familiar.

Pity the eye that sees no more in the sun than a
stove to keep it warm and a torch to light its way between the home and the business office. That is a
blind eye, even if capable of seeing a fly a mile away.
Pity the ear that hears no more than so many notes in
the song of the nightingale. It is a deaf ear, even if
capable of hearing the crawling of ants in their sub-
terranean labyrinths.[29]

Speaking with Mary Haskell on symbolic meanings,
Gibran stated that the purpose of art is to reveal the essence
of the natural symbol "by means of other, more suggestive
symbols."[30] Gibran said that man has never actually seen
God, yet man sees God with the eye of the imagination.
If man were an imaginary being, he would have no need for
symbols. But man lives in a sensory world, "and it is quite

[29] Naimy, pp. 62-63.
[30] *Ibid.*, p. 58.

impossible for imagination to make itself real to the senses unless it clothe itself in shapes and forms perceivable to the senses."[31]

Referring to the picture, "The Soul's Return to God," Gibran said that once the face is seen with the eye, the next step is to see it with the imagination. One is to look for the attributes of godhood. In accord with one's own knowledge, perhaps one can see more than he, Gibran, has put into the face. He pointed to a shaft of light rising from the bottom of the picture and told Miss Haskell that now she should have no difficulty in seeing in it a soul returning to God after death.

> "Art must be a direct communication between the artist's imagination and that of the looker. For that reason, I avoid, so much as possible, busying the looker's eye with too many details in order that his imagination may roam wide and far. As to the physical molds, art is forced to create for expressing itself; they must be beautiful molds. Otherwise, art defeats its purpose."[32]

Miss Haskell then asked why he always drew the bodies naked. Gibran answered,

> "Because life is naked. A nude body is the truest and noblest symbol of life. If I draw a mountain as a heap of human forms or paint a waterfall in the shape of tumbling human bodies, it is because I see in the mountain a heap of living things, and in the waterfall a precipitate current of life."[33]

Rodin said that art "is the pleasure of the mind which searches into Nature and which there divines the spirit by which Nature is animated."[34] And art is the sublime

[31] Ibid.
[32] Ibid.
[33] Ibid., p. 59.
[34] Rodin, op.cit., p. 29.

mission of man, "since it is the expression of thought seek-
ing to understand the world and to make it understood."[35]

Gibran felt that "every person is potentially an
artist."[36] He said,

A child may be taught to draw a bird as easily as to
write the word. He may make rhymes while he is
learning to make sentences, and he may model clay
when he learns to build with his first blocks.[37]

Gibran knew what the value of art could be to man,
and he also knew the value of his own art. When Gibran
was asked to sign his drawings, he laughed and said, "No!
Why should? It will still be known for a Gibran when
I have lain long in the good dark earth beneath the
cedars."[38]

Miss Raphael said that although Gibran was a native
of Lebanon, he is neither of the East nor of the West but
"a citizen of the land of Cosmopolis—that ever-moving
realm, somewhat like the fabled island of Atlantis, which
belongs to all times and to no particular place."[39]

Gibran is not only interested in present-day man; he
is interested in the history of life and the struggles in life.
In his first collection of drawings in book form, Gibran
presented his impressions of man as he struggles with the
forces of life. The following eight drawings are taken from
Twenty Drawings.[40] These selections are chosen to exemplify Gibran's early drawings, the only ones not accompanied with his writings but which, nevertheless, can be
related to concepts expressed in much of his writings.

[35] Ibid., p. 30.
[36] Young, p. 10.
[37] Ibid.
[38] Ibid., p. 24.
[39] Twenty Drawings, p. 2.
[40] Reproduced from Twenty Drawings by Kahlil Gibran, by permission
of the publisher, Alfred A. Knopf, Inc. Copyright 1919 by Alfred A.
Knopf, Inc.

TOWARD THE INFINITE

Gibran portrays the profile of a woman with head thrust forward in her eagerness to reach toward the Infinite. The hair is forced back, away from the face. The lips are sensitive and determined. Bruises are seen on the flesh of the face and neck. Yet with eyes partially closed, indifferent to her pain, she surges forth toward her goal.

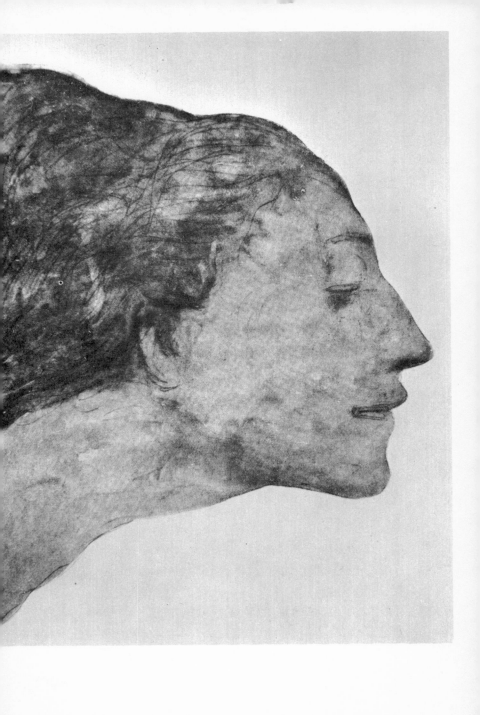

THE GREAT LONGING

All the strength, vigor, and force of man's dual nature cannot release him from his bondage to earth. The human in him aspires to the height. Even though the animal in him helps the human effort, the mission cannot entirely succeed. Man is ever bound to earth, yet he persists in his longing for the spiritual.

THE ROCK

It is as though a fist were thrust forth and became a rock. Human heads take on the form of knuckles and bodies become durable flesh. Gibran said,

> You and the stone are one. There is only a difference in heart-beats. Your heart beats a little faster, does it, my friend? Ay, but it is not so tranquil.[41]

The stone is part of creation just as man is. The rock is shown as part of something unseen. The drawing exemplifies the relatedness and durability of life.

[41] *The Garden of the Prophet*, p. 36.

COMPASSION

Woman is pictured in her dual personality. Sympathy and compassion arrest the strong and rough nature of the animal. Woman's body, small and impressionable, bends low to express love to suffering humanity.

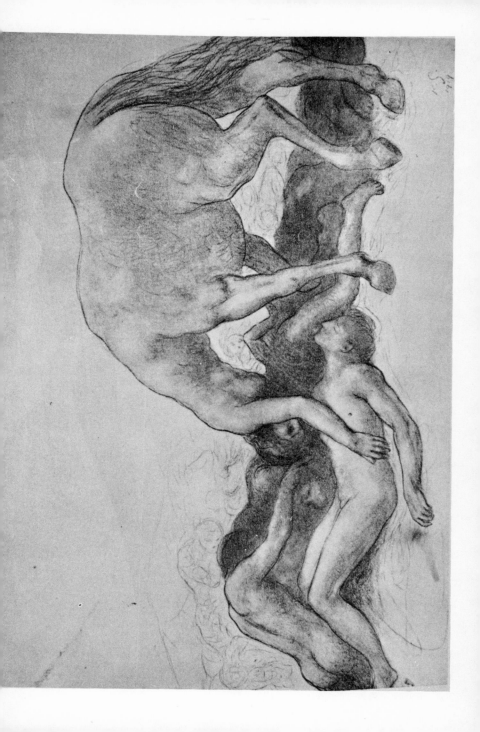

THE STRUGGLE

Woman is pictured frantically clinging to the body of man for comfort and support. She is completely dependent on him and lifts her legs off the ground clasping them about the man. The man pushes her away with one hand and embraces her head with the other. However, his clasp is free and his countenance exhibits his quiet understanding. The struggle and agony involved bespeak the Crucifixion.

CRUCIFIED

Here a woman with arms outstretched is held by two men. Three bodies form the symbol of suffering. The woman is torn apart in her love for two men, invariably experiencing the agony of pain. The men are relegated to the background of the drawing, suggesting that the choice is the woman's.

THE INNERMOST

Standing on one leg bent at the knee touching the earth, man is bowed in his resolve to plumb the innermost self. All man's physical and mental abilities are directed inward in an effort to understand the inner life of the spirit.

The small figure is perhaps a preliminary sketch by the artist.

THE GREATER SELF

Man's small nature is held tenderly by his greater nature. The embrace is not confining; man is free to search for his greater self. Man's head is bent and covered, so to speak, with his own blindness. His greater self is ever near, but man does not see it.

The Prophet is Gibran's masterpiece. It contains his philosophy of life developed over a period of approximately twelve years. Twelve years is also the time the prophet, Almustufa, spent in the city of Orphalese. Now he must leave. Before he leaves, and at the people's request, he speaks to them on various aspects of life. The subject discussed here accompanied by drawings treats themes of love, marriage, children; giving, the larger self, and the "Creative Hand."[42] The drawings have been chosen because they are additional reflections on the spiritual essence of man relative to himself and others.

The titles of the interpretations are taken from the selections in which the drawings are placed, with the exception of the "Creative Hand."

[42] The following six photographs are reproduced from *The Prophet*, by Kahlil Gibran, by permission of the publisher, Alfred A. Knopf, Inc. Copyright 1923 by Kahlil Gibran; renewal copyright 1951 by Administrators C. T. A. of Kahlil Gibran Estate, and Mary G. Gibran.

ON LOVE

Love gives naught but itself and takes naught
                                    but from itself.
Love possesses not nor would it be possessed;
For love is sufficient unto love.[43]

The figures of the man and woman appear to embrace each other without binding each other in any manner. The hands are free; there is only a slight touch of the woman's hand on the man's body.

[43] *The Prophet*, p. 13.

ON MARRIAGE

Give your hearts, but not into each others's keeping.

For only the hand of Life can contain your hearts.

And stand together yet not too near together:

For the pillars of the temple stand apart,

And the oak tree and the cypress grow not in each other's shadow.[44]

The All-Mother extends her hand up from earth to separate the man from the woman. They hold hands, exemplifying their union and their dependence on each other, yet there remains enough space for separate growth and freedom.

[44] *The Prophet*, p. 16.

ON CHILDREN

You are the bows from which your children as living arrows are sent forth.

The archer sees the mark upon the path of the Infinite, and He bends you with His might that His arrows may go swift and far.

Let your bending in the archer's hand be for gladness;

For even as He loves the arrow that flies, so He loves also the bow that is stable.[45]

The archer represents Life, the bow the parents, and the arrow which has been released, the child. Parents must relinquish their children to the fortunes of life with gladness, for Life smiles on those that are flexible, flexibility being a form of stability.

[45] *The Prophet,* p. 18.

ON GIVING

And there are those who give and know not pain
in giving, nor do they seek joy, nor give with mindful-
ness of virtue;
They give as in yonder valley the myrtle breathes
its fragrance into space.
Through the hands of such as these God speaks,
and from behind their eyes He smiles upon the earth.[46]

The feminine body is portrayed in its primordial in-
nocence. It is the gift of self given fearlessly, asking no
return. It is love of the highest form, and in its giving
bestows joy on both the giver and the receiver.

[46] *The Prophet*, p. 20.

THE LARGER SELF

You are not enclosed within your bodies, nor con-
fined to houses or fields.
That which is you dwells above the mountain and
roves with the wind.
It is not a thing that crawls into the sun for
warmth or digs holes into darkness for safety,
But a thing free, a spirit that envelops the earth
and moves in the ether.[47]

Man is pictured with arms stretched away from the
body forming a cross and reaching upward towards his
larger self. He seeks his spiritual self, which is always near
but ever free to roam the earth untouched by the physical
elements.

[47] The Prophet, pp. 91-92.

THE CREATIVE HAND

The final drawing represents the farewell of the prophet, who says:

What was given us here we shall keep,
And if it suffices not, then again must we come
together and together stretch our hands unto the
giver.[48]

The hand represents the hand of God, the All-Feeling and All-Seeing. Angels' wings in a whirling circular movement encircle the hand, lending a touch of mystery and fantasy. Human forms encircle the whole, separated from the hand by a dark abyss. This chaotic area is spanned on either side by the misty forms of wings as they are hurled frantically from the center. It is the life cycle which is the creation, the struggle, death, and the return again to life.

[48] *The Prophet*, p. 94.

The Earth Gods is a long prose poem in which three voices, representing three gods, state their views on man and his destiny. The First God is tired of ruling over man and wants to be relieved of his burden. The Second God is ambitious still to rule man, for he thinks man is weak and needs to be ruled. The Third God has seen a young couple singing and dancing in the forest of love's first awakening. The Third God tells of his discovery, but the others do not hear him. Finally, when they do turn their attention to his urgent call, they see the young couple and concede that love is upon the earth and they are content. The following seven photographs[49] illustrate the thoughts of the three Earth Gods. The captions are derived from the chosen selections, with the exception of "The Fountain of Pain."

[49] Reproduced from *The Earth Gods*, by Kahlil Gibran, by permission of the publisher, Alfred A. Knopf, Inc. Copyright 1931 by Kahlil Gibran; renewal copyright 1951 by Administrators C. T. A. of Kahlil Gibran Estate, and Mary G. Gibran.

THE MARRIAGE

The Second God is relating the story of Creation; he says:

> And unto earth came life, and unto life came the spirit, the winged melody of the universe. And we ruled life and spirit, and none save us knew the measure of the years nor the weight of years' nebulous dreams, till we, at noontide of the seventh aeon, gave the sea in marriage to the sun.[50]

In this drawing the winged masculine flame of the sun touches the feminine form of the sea. The two spirits of life are thus united, and out of their union man is born.

[50] *The Earth Gods*, p. 15.

MAN'S SERVITUDE

The lark calls to the lark,
But upward the eagle soars,
Nor tarries to hear the song.
You would teach me self love fulfilled
*   in man's worship,*
And content with man's servitude.[51]

The First God denounces man's servitude to his past. There is a procession of fearful, bewildered, naked bodies moving towards the entrance of a cavern. Outside are snakes crawling near them. Not knowing what to do in their Garden of Eden, they choose the darkness of the cave, the symbol of their dark traditions. Above them is another procession, birds flying freely in the open sky exposed to all the physical elements of nature. But they are free.

[51] *The Earth Gods,* p. 17.

WRACK OF MAN

Does dawn hold the heart of night unto her heart?
Or shall the sea heed the bodies of her dead?
Like dawn my soul rises within me
Naked and unencumbered.
And like the unresting sea
My heart casts out a perishing wrack of man and
earth.[52]

The First God relates man's earthly condition. Bodies are shown thrown carelessly and indiscriminately onto the shore of life. It is a chaotic world, and man is suffering because of his plight. In the background the nebulous mist gives way to the bare entrance of light illuminating the bodies. The picture exemplifies the indifference of the forces of nature toward men.

[52] *The Earth Gods*, p. 26.

MOTHER EARTH

Behold, man and woman
Flame to flame,
In white ecstasy.
Roots that suck at the breast of purple earth,
Flame flowers at the breasts of the sky.
And we are the purple breast,
And we are the enduring sky.[53]

The Third God is beginning to be heard. Men and women are endowed with fire, which is representative of warmth and joy. They are as roots receiving their nourishment from majestic earth. They develop rising up as flowers in the open sky. Men and women thus become part of Mother Earth, the symbol of the three Earth Gods.

[53] *The Earth Gods*, p. 31.

PASSION

Now then, I come, and coming I offer up
My passion and my pain.
Lo, there is the dancer, carved out of our
ancient eagerness,
And the singer is crying mine own songs unto
the wind.
And in that dancing and in that singing
A god is slain within me.[54]

The First God becomes aware of the singer and the
dancer. He sees that the same love which emanates from
the young is inherent in him also. His weariness is overcome, and in his passion and pain the god of his lower
self is slain. The spirit of love hovers over the heads of the
young couple, touching them and blessing them.

[54] *The Earth Gods*, p. 36.

THE FOUNTAIN OF PAIN

Love is our lord and master.
It is not a wanton decay of the flesh,
Nor the crumbling of desire
When desire and self are wrestling;
Nor is it flesh that takes arms against
*   the spirit.*
Love rebels not.[55]

The Third God describes what love is not. Bodies are portrayed as if they were the waters of a fountain which rise up to meet the sky, but invariably fall to come again to itself again and again. Love is not found in rebellion against oneself, nor is it discovered in reckless self destruction. Love comes to light when the spirit is at peace.

[55] *The Earth Gods,* p. 37.

THE BLESSED FORGE

The blessed forge burns,
The sparks rise, and each spark is a sun.
Better it is for us, and wiser,
To seek a shadowed nook and sleep in our
  earth divinity,
And let love, human and frail, command
  the coming day.[56]

The Third God bestows the final benediction on man.
The Earth Gods are thus relegated to a minor position,
giving way to Love as expressed in the relations of human
life.

[56] *The Earth Gods,* pp. 40-41.

Gibran's art, like his literary parables, is related directly to life experiences and life's spiritual essence. Life is the power that moves the universe, and man shares in this living power. Even though man is a human being, he partakes of the characteristics of the animal. Man is also in a constant state of longing. If his longing is not properly understood, man suffers conflicts and pain. Much of man's suffering comes from his misunderstanding of natural life processes. He builds dark caves for shelter, symbolic of his limiting practices. Yet the forces of nature from which he attempts to escape are indifferent to man. The warmth of the sun and the violence of the tempest touch all men. It is left to man to harmonize his thinking and his action with the existent spiritual elements of the universe. Out of that harmony, beauty and love are born. Then man can truly say with Gibran, "let love, human and frail, command the coming day."

Thus, Gibran's spiritual messages to mankind have been shown to exist in both his art and his writings. An interpretation of his art has been attempted to correlate the two aspects of his gifts and to reveal the symbolic expressions of his art as analogous to the parabolic form of his writings. Gibran's concern was never so much with the material as with the spiritual world that man silently inhabits. It is important that man should know more about the spiritual aspect of his character. Then he can also come to know more about the material aspect. If by the expressions of his thoughts, Gibran is able to awaken others to an awareness of their thoughts, his mission will be fulfilled.

4

The Spirit of Man

GIBRAN'S PARABLES IN prose and art aim directly
at the expression of the spiritual inner life of man. His
thinking is simple and easily understood. His intentions
are aimed toward the awakening of man's spiritual awareness that is inherent in life experiences. He establishes no
specific pattern of behavior, philosophy, or ethics. Once,
he was asked for definite rules of conduct for a consistent
and orderly life. Gibran replied, "I lay down no rules of
conduct. Do whatsoever you will so long as you do it
beautifully."[1] Upon being asked about religion, he said,

"Religion? What is it? I know only life. Life means
the field, the vineyard and the loom . . . The Church
is within you. You yourself are your priest."

And again on the same subject: "Religion among
men is but a field tilled by those who have a purpose;
some hopeful for the bliss of eternity, some ignorant,
fearful of future flame."

And still again: "All that is worth while is a free

[1] Young, p. 38.

spirit. *And this means as many different things as there are different human beings.*"[2]

To Gibran, then, man is his own church, with the power of being his own priest. Religion limits men to a particular doctrine whereas life is unlimited; life includes all things: the open field, the cultivated vineyard, and the loom or factory. Moreover, the only thing worth while is a free spirit, which is open to grasp and to understand all things. Although a free spirit means something different to each individual, a state of freedom embodies a state of awareness of the meaning of life experiences. It is contemplation in its highest form. It is what Gibran called "spiritual chemistry" or "communion in space."[3] He said,

> I believe that there are groups of people and individuals the world over who are kin regardless of race. They are in the same realm of consciousness. This is kinship, only this.[4]

This concept is far reaching. The "same realm of consciousness" is a unifying principle which operates toward a harmonious relationship between man and man. It is harmony which creates the beautiful in thought and deed. "There is neither religion nor science beyond beauty,"[5] Gibran said. The creation of beauty is analogous to the creation of "a living, invisible force which will survive and create in its turn."[6] This living force is like a song or a poem that shall not die. In one of his poems, Gibran has a youth say to a sage who laments the condition of man:

[2] *Ibid.*
[3] *Ibid.*, p. 131.
[4] *Ibid.*, p. 168.
[5] Kahlil Gibran, *Sand and Foam* (New York: Alfred A. Knopf, 1926), p. 55.
[6] *Ibid.*, p. 132.

> *Give to me the reed and sing thou!*
> *Forget all the cures and ills,*
> *Mankind is like verses written*
> *Upon the surface of the rills.*[7]

In his last book, published posthumously, Gibran wrote that the earth heaved man a song and a riddle; "a song unto the sky, a riddle unto the earth; and what is there between earth and sky that shall carry the song and solve the riddle save our own passion."[8] Man, therefore, is born with dual potentialities. He is at one with his spiritual essence and a riddle or a problem in his earthy life, and the only solution that harmonizes these two aspects of his character is his passion, which is the inherent flame of love.

Man's passionate living force is described in still another way by E. M. Forster, one of England's distinguished writers, as a collective "shy crablike sideways movement," one of two movements of the human mind; the other being the "great tedious onrush known as history."[9] There is a possibility for this movement to gain momentum if human nature can be altered. However, Forster says,

> *If human nature does alter it will be because individuals manage to look at themselves in a new way. Here and there people—a few people . . . —are trying to do this. Every institution and vested interest is against such a search: organized religion, the state, the family in its economic aspect, have nothing to gain,*

---

[7] Kahlil Gibran, *The Processions*, trans. George Kheirallah (New York: The Philosophical Library, 1958), p. 73.

[8] Kahlil Gibran, *The Garden of the Prophet* (New York: Alfred A. Knopf, 1933), p. 3.

[9] E. M. Forster, *Aspects of the Novel* (New York: Harcourt, Brace and Company, 1954), p. 173.

*and it is only when outward prohibitions weaken that
it can proceed: history conditions it to that extent.*[10]

One might say Gibran was one of the few people who
managed to look at himself in a new way. Many people
recognized this difference in him and during his lifetime
sought his help and guidance. Barbara Young says,

> Every day of his days for many years, his high room,
> quiet and simple in the heart of the big city, had been
> the last station on the journey of a multitude of pil-
> grims. Little the world knew, because he did not wish
> it to know, that hour after hour, day after day, the feet
> of many sought him, eager and weary and hopeful.
> Many a time his own weariness exceeded the need of
> those who came, yet he did not turn them away.[11]

Gibran knew of the great longing of mankind toward
self-realization. Man's longing, his silent need, manifested
itself in a multiplicity of forms, but these forms were "all
on the way"[12] to man's spiritual unfolding. For the Spirit
of man is in man. It is his inner faculty that must be
recognized. In a voice transplanted from the East, which,
however, recognized no particular province as its own,
Gibran said:

> I came to say a word and shall utter it. Should death
> take me ere I give voice, the morrow shall utter it.
> For the morrow leaves not a secret hidden in the book
> of the Infinite.[13]

[10] *Ibid.*, pp. 172-173.
[11] Young, p. 127-128.
[12] *Ibid.*, p. 39.
[13] Kahlil Gibran, *A Tear and A Smile*, trans. H. M. Nahmad (New
York: Alfred A. Knopf, 1950), p. 197.

Bibliography

A. PRIMARY SOURCES

Gibran, Kahlil. *Broken Wings.* Trans. Anthony R. Ferris. New York: The Citadel Press, 1957.
———. *Earth Gods.* New York: Alfred A. Knopf, 1931.
———. *The Forerunner.* New York: Alfred A. Knopf, 1920.
———. *The Garden of the Prophet.* New York: Alfred A. Knopf, 1933.
———. *Jesus the Son of Man.* New York: Alfred A. Knopf, 1928.
———. *The Madman.* New York: Alfred A. Knopf, 1918.
———. *Nymphs of the Valley.* Trans. H. M. Nahmad. New York: Alfred A. Knopf, 1948.
———. *The Processions.* Trans. George Kheirallah. New York: The Philosophical Library, 1958.
———. *The Prophet.* New York: Alfred A. Knopf, 1923.
———. *Prose Poems.* Trans. Andrew Grareeb. New York: Alfred A. Knopf, 1934.
———. *Sand and Foam.* New York: Alfred A. Knopf, 1926.
———. *Secrets of the Heart.* Trans. Anthony R. Ferris. New York: The Philosophical Library, 1947.
———. *Spirits Rebellious.* Trans. H. M. Nahmad. New York: Alfred A. Knopf, 1948.

————. *A Tear and A Smile*. Trans. H. M. Nahmad. New York: Alfred A. Knopf, 1950.

————. *Tears and Laughter*. Trans. Anthony R. Ferris. New York: The Philosophical Library, 1949.

————. *Thoughts and Meditations*. Trans. Anthony R. Ferris. New York: The Citadel Press, 1960.

————. *Treasury of Kahlil Gibran*. Trans. Anthony R. Ferris. New York: The Citadel Press, 1951.

————. *Twenty Century Drawings*. New York: Alfred A. Knopf, 1919.

————. *Voice of the Master*. Trans. Anthony R. Ferris. New York: The Citadel Press, 1958.

————. *The Wanderer*. New York: Alfred A. Knopf, 1932.

B. BIOGRAPHIES AND LETTERS

Gibran, Kahlil. *A Self Portrait*. Trans. Anthony R. Ferris. New York: The Citadel Press, 1959.

Naimy, Mikhail. *Kahlil Gibran: A Biography*. New York: The Philosophical Library, 1950.

Young, Barbara. *This Man from Lebanon*. New York: Alfred A. Knopf, 1945.

C. SECONDARY SOURCES

Bragdon, C. F. "Modern Prophet from Lebanon," *Merely Players*. New York: Alfred A. Knopf, 1929.

Knopf, Alfred A. "News Release," letter dated November 21, 1961.

Lecerf, Jean. "Djabran Khalil Djabran et les origines de la prose poétique moderne." *Orient*. No. 3 (1957), pp. 7-14.

Ross, Martha Jean. "The Writings of Kahlil Gibran." Unpublished Master's thesis, The University of Texas, Austin, 1948.

Russell, G. W. "Kahlil Gibran," *Living Torch*. New York: Macmillan Company, 1938.

D. OTHER WORKS CONSULTED

Blakney, Raymond B. (trans.). *Meister Eckhart.* New York: Harper and Brothers (Harper Torchbooks), 1957.

Clouston, W. A. (ed.). *Arabian Poetry.* Glasgow: M'Laren and Sons, 1881.

Cohen, J. M. *Robert Browning.* New York: Longman's, Green and Company, 1952.

Curtius, Ernst Robert. *European Literature and the Latin Middle Ages.* New York: Pantheon Books, Inc., 1953.

Donne, John. "xvii. Meditation," *Seventeenth-Century Prose and Poetry,* Robert P. Tristram Coffin and Alexander M. Witherspoon, eds. New York: Harcourt, Brace and Company, 1946.

Emerson, Ralph Waldo. "The Poet," *American Heritage,* vol. 1. Leon Howard, Louis B. Wright, and Carl Bode, eds. Boston: D.C. Heath and Company, 1955.

Filas, Francis. *The Parables of Jesus.* New York: The Macmillan Company, 1959.

Forster, E. M. *Aspects of the Novel.* New York: Harcourt Brace and Company (Harvest Books), 1954.

Frazer, Sir James George. *The Golden Bough.* New York: The Macmillan Company, 1947.

Fromm, Erich. *Escape from Freedom.* New York: Holt, Rinehart and Winston, 1941.

Guillaumont, A., and others (translators). *The Gospel According to Thomas.* New York: Harper and Brothers, 1959.

Hamady, Sania. *Temperament and Character of the Arabs.* New York: Twayne Publishers, 1960.

Ibn Khaldun. *The Muqaddimah, An Introduction to History.* Trans. Franz Rosenthal. 3 vols. New York: Bollingen Foundation, Inc., 1958.

Jordan, E. *Essays in Criticism.* Chicago: University of Chicago Press, 1952.

"Lao Tzu," *Encyclopedia Britannica* (27 ed.), xii, page 712.

Nicholson, R. A. *A Literary History of the Arabs.* New York: Cambridge University Press, 1956.

Nietzsche, Friedrich. "Thus Spake Zarathustra," *The Philoso-phy of Nietzsche*. Trans. Thomas Common. New York: The Modern Library, 1954.
Rodin, Auguste. *On Art and Artists*. New York: The Philo-sophical Library, 1957.
Taylor, William M. *The Parables of Our Saviour*. New York: Doubleday, Doran and Company, Inc., 1929.
Zolondek, Leon. *Di'bil b. 'Ali, The Life and Writings of an Early Abbasid Poet*. Kentucky: University of Kentucky Press, 1961.